The FUTURE of INEQUALITY

The
FUTURE
of
INEQUALITY

S. M. Miller
eymour *ichael*

and

Pamela A. Roby

BASIC BOOKS, INC., PUBLISHERS
New York / London

TO RICHARD M. TITMUSS, MARTIN REIN, AND BERTRAM GROSS

Preface

This is a book about people; this is a book full of data. These two contentions do not conflict, for the data we cite are one way of understanding the social relations among individuals and the kinds of lives that they lead. While we have made a dispassionate presentation and analysis of inequality, we are impelled to our task by the urgency of reducing inequalities. We see people in the tables. Percentages, ratios, and Gini coefficients do not obscure the fact that real, suffering people are involved, and that the character of their interrelationships is always central.

In this book we do not argue the reasons why inequality should be reduced. For one, it is difficult to be more eloquent and moving than R. H. Tawney.* For another, the 1960's should have made it uncomfortably clear to most Americans that black and Spanish-speaking citizens are demanding equality and have a strong

---

* R. H. Tawney, *Equality* (New York: Capricorn Books, 1931). In a book now in preparation tentatively entitled *Poverty and Education* we will deal with the necessity of reducing inequalities if social mobility is to be promoted.

case. And we think that, among the poor and "the other, other America" of whites on the margins of affluence, gnawing and growing doubts are emerging about the equity of the current distribution of the output and satisfactions of our society.

Consequently, we have not forged the book around the issue of the blacks alone. While we do highlight the inequalities of the blacks, our concern is broader—to view the position of all Americans, especially those who, in terms of income, are the bottom 20 per cent (of whom one-fourth are black). To understand the relative standing of the bottom, the well-being of the rest of society must also be gauged.

The issues of inequality are broad. In recent years, the rekindling of economists' interest in questions of inequality has been an important gain. But economists have dominated the discussion and reduced inequality to income alone. We think it is necessary to see inequality in more than economic terms (and even in economic terms, in ways broader than those adopted by many economists); the task of Part I is a broader conceptualization of inequalities and an analysis of trends.

In this analysis, as a byproduct of our major effort, we have tried to depict the social indicators that could measure progress or retardation in the reduction of inequalities. While we are concerned with better governmental collection of data, we are even more concerned that independent groups collect and assay important data in terms of the goal of reduction of inequalities. We do not accept some "New Left" criticisms of social indicators as inevitably establishment-supporting. Better data can lead to better analyses and criticism—and that is our objective.

Part II is concerned with the issues now emerging in American society, issues that will be central if our society makes a major commitment to reducing inequalities in the 1970's. Since our affluence is mortgaged to military and lunar activity and consumer profligacy, our political system to ineffective forms, and our way of life to quantity, not quality, it may be difficult to reduce inequalities, extend freedom, and promote authenticity in personal relations during the next decade.

Where are the hopes for a better world? They lie in increased recognition of the difficulties, inequities, and costs of this one; in the emergence of insurgent groups concerned about change; and in the growing dissatisfaction of a wide variety of Americans with the lives that they lead. Although not yet a political coalition, frequently foolhardy, compulsively disruptive and schismatic, a convergence of the poor, the black, the students, the marginal whites, and the disaffected professionals is possible. They do not share one common agenda, but there can be sufficient convergence at points. What they lack is a program. We hope this book provides analysis and data that can lead to a program.

New York   S.M.M.
January 1970   P.A.R.

Personal Acknowledgments

The intellectual progenitor of this book is Richard Titmuss of the London School of Economics. His seminal essay on "The Social Division of Welfare"* opened our eyes to the various components of economic well-being. Martin Rein and Bertram Gross, friends and collaborators, widened our vision. Earlier versions of ideas in this book appeared in articles co-authored with them, and we appreciate their willingness to see these ideas become imbedded here.

Many others gave us leads to data, provided us with data, helped us understand the problems with which we were grappling, or criticized our interpretations. Among them are Herrington J. Bryce, O. D. Duncan, Elizabeth Durbin, Sar Levitan, Charlotte Muller, Oscar Ornati, Mollie Orshansky, and Israel Putnam. Janet Amidon, Margaret Kimple, and Silvia Suarez rapidly and carefully typed drafts of the manuscript.

* Published as Chapter 2 of his *Essays on the Welfare State* (New Haven: Yale University Press, 1959).

x

If Richard Titmuss is the intellectual source of this study, foundations are the financial. In a time of public pillorying of foundations from right and left, we want to acknowledge our indebtedness to them for encouraging us to "do our thing" as well as we could. The foundations bet on us and the likelihood of our developing our ideas in useful ways when these ideas were very inchoate. We hope that their confidence has not been misplaced.

The project that produced this book began with a flexible grant offered by the Stern Family Fund and its open-minded director, David R. Hunter. It was continued on a grant from the Ford Foundation, which was initiated by the innovative director of its then Public Affairs Division, Paul N. Ylvisaker, and his colleague, Henry Saltzman, who have inspired, guided, and aided many others. When one of us, S. M. Miller, joined the staff of the Ford Foundation for two years, John Coleman, Louis Winnick, and later Mitchell Sviridoff of the Foundation made it possible for him to continue some work on the project. Both the Ford Foundation and the Stern Family Fund encouraged us to try out new ideas, were resourceful in making funds flexible, and disassociated themselves from the project itself so that we had complete freedom. While neither foundation is responsible for what emerged, what has been developed is largely due to the generous and flexible support without constraints that we enjoyed. May other investigators have such good fortune!

The Miller family—Jean, Jon, and Ned—have contributed to this book through their indulgence with neglect, vigilance for the protection of an author's time, and joint concern for the disadvantaged. Jean's concern with inequality and emotional problems has deepened our awareness of the human dimensions of inequality. We are also grateful to Zelma Oole, Elmer Jacobson, and Arthur Shirey, three dedicated teachers, to the leaders of "P.F." who first introduced one of us to the strengths and needs of the blacks and the poor, and to Marianna and Clark Roby for making it possible to come in contact with these people.

S.M.M.
P.A.R.

A personal note:

When a younger person writes with an older one, it is customary to regard the younger as the junior author. In this and our other writings, junior-senior is inappropriate terminology. We are joint authors. The arranging of names on the title page is a tribute to the alphabet, not to hierarchy or contribution.

SMM

Contents

PART I

From
Poverty
to
Inequality

1
From Poverty to Inequality

Poverty has become the acceptable way of discussing the more disturbing issue of inequality. Poverty has not been fully recognized as the shorthand for the much broader idea because the historic subsistence connotations of the term still survive. As a result, we have heated debates that fail to clarify issues or touch the real problems of the poor. For some, it will come as a shock to learn that their words are the prose of inequality; for others, their statements will surprise them when parsed into nineteenth-century sensibilities about pauperism.

The "discovery" of poverty in the United States did not take place because part of the population lived in worse circumstances than in previous generations. Some of those characterized as poor do live in as difficult conditions as the poor of previous generations or the

3

poor of Calcutta. But by and large that is not the situation of poverty in high-income, industrial nations today. Some contemporary "poor," as emphasized in the late 1960's, are hungry or dwell in shelters that are inadequate for physical survival, but this is not typical. Nor are most of those who are classified as being "in poverty" paupers or dependents whose only financial support comes from government.

Nonetheless, worsened conditions, threatened physical survival, and pauperism, singly or together, characterize the historic concern with poverty. In the United States' desperate depression of the 1930's, a decline in living standards was the issue. In low-income societies, physical survival is often threatened; in nineteenth-century England, pauperism was the focus.

Today, within the high-income industrial societies, these are not the main difficulties. The growing and groping concern with poverty in these societies results from revelations about inequality. The euphoria of economic growth that followed World War II overwhelmed any doubts about the quality of materialism. Economic justice was not an issue in the 1950's, for there was confidence that all in society, especially those at the bottom, were benefiting from expansion. The bigger economic pie was yielding relatively larger slices to the bottommost groups. Social problems were interpreted as gracefully succumbing to the mighty power of economic growth.

Gradually, however, a disturbing recognition upset affluent complacency. The problems of those at the

4

bottom had not been eradicated. The proportion of national income obtained by the bottom group probably did not increase in the United States or in most other economies following World War II.

Old standards of well-being no longer apply. New forms of division and stratification are emerging. A man's car or washing machine does not assure him decent housing, full citizenship in society, nor his children equal access to decent jobs and education.

Obviously the lack of full economic or social citizenship in society is different from the condition of poverty in which families are starving. In the affluent society, relative deprivation, a comparative position of losing out, characterizes most of those termed poor. The historic term, poverty, once applied to low-income families in industrializing societies is found wanting when stretched to highly industrialized societies.

Poverty, then, has surreptitiously ushered in the issue of inequality in the affluent society. To examine poverty is to examine American society and its changes. A thorough analysis of poverty must confront the level of living of the nonpoor with that of the poor. As the late Polish sociologist Stanislaw Ossowski wrote in his trenchant analysis of social stratification, ". . . a class [is] a member of a certain system of relations. This means that the definition of any class must take into account the relation of this group to other groups in this system."[1] *Not only the poor but the entire society is at issue today.* Lagging incomes rather than low incomes are the issue.

The inequality perspective demands that poverty programs be recognized as efforts to engineer changes in the stratification profiles of the United States. To be deeply and frontally concerned about inequalities is to address the divisions and stratifications in society: How great should the economic and social differences be among various groups in society? What are the bases of monetary and status rewards? In what ways can the mechanisms that disburse rewards be changed? In attempting to obtain these changes, how much controversy and agitation is desirable or acceptable?

Not all agree on the new agenda. Some argue that to broaden the definition of poverty is to downgrade the attention to income. But we do not think diminished emphasis on income is inevitable—as we demonstrate in succeeding chapters. Those who discuss the issues of poverty are divided on the important question of how wide the gap between groups must be before it is deemed significant and undesirable. Some argue for the desirability of placing the income poverty line at a low level in order to discourage dependency or governmental activity which might interfere with market forces. Nonetheless, even proponents of these approaches are concerned with relativities. They adjust the income poverty line to changes in the general standard of living, though at a slower rate than those who would more frankly embrace a relative approach.

The social-welfare term *poverty* does not incur the disturbance of the political term *inequality*, but the ambiguity of the term poverty does prevent the badly

6

needed, full-scale examination of the issues of inequality: Who gets what? Who does and should benefit from government subsidization? What should be the shape of the income and social profiles of this country?

These difficult questions produce acrimonious debate. Obviously, adherence to the historic view of poverty leads to social policies and social indicators that are inadequate for the problems generated by inequalities. Furthermore, it is much easier to show progress in social achievement when a historic fixed income is employed as a poverty standard. If standards were based upon relativities, there might exist the politically embarrassing situation of nonexistent progress. The absence of achievement when these indicators of inequality are the measure would lead many officials to argue for a different concept of poverty. Many policy critics, on the other hand, would advocate the use of the inequality indicators and the augmentation of the resources that are allocated to the underclass. Thus, the conceptualization of the problem of poverty and the choice of social indicators can be in the service of political objectives and constraints. For example, Mollie Orshansky has recently noted some interesting aspects of the development of the "SSA poverty line." She recalls:

At the Social Security Administration, we decided that we would develop two measures of need, and state, on the basis of the income sample of the Current Population Survey, how many and what kinds of families these measures de-

7

lineated. It was not the Social Security Administration that labeled the poverty line. It remained for the Office of Economic Opportunity and the Council of Economic Advisors to select the lower of the two measures and decide they would use it as the working tool. . . . It is interesting that few outside the Social Security Administration ever wanted to talk about the higher measure. Everybody wanted only to talk about the lower one, labeled the "poverty line," which yielded roughly the same number of people in poverty as the original $3,000 measure did, except that fewer families with more children were substituted for a larger number of older families without children.[2]

This kind of situation argues for the importance of multiple conceptualizations and producers of social indicators of progress and problems. In our view, not all users of indicators have the same needs: indicators can be used for spotting problems and unmet needs, detecting trends and their changes, or assessing policies; they may primarily serve the interests of low-income, working, middle- or upper-income groups. Much of the contemporary discussion of indicators is in terms of the policy operators, not the outsiders—the independent, external, critical groups. The needs of official agencies for social indicators of poverty may be different, for example, from those of civil rights groups. In the first part of this book we are more concerned with examining the issues of poverty and inequality from the perspective of the nongovernmental groups which represent the poor than from the viewpoint of official agencies.[3]

POVERTY: AN INCOME OR A SOCIAL CONDITION?

Much of the current discussion of poverty is posed in terms of an income line: How many families and individuals live below this line, adjusted for family size and other conditions? At what rate is this number being reduced? The availability of these figures and the historic view of poverty in terms of pauperism leads to an emphasis on the income figures. But today income is only *one* dimension of poverty and inequality.

In the last third of the twentieth century we need new approaches for analyzing and developing the quality of life. A stratificational analysis is required, which not only views the poor as those who are lagging behind relative to others in society, but which extends the concept of poverty beyond the narrow limits of income to the qualities of political and personal relations. Max Weber and Richard Titmuss have already made major contributions to the needed analysis. One of Weber's outstanding contributions to social science lies in his untwining of the three components of stratification: class, status, and power.[4] The Marxist analysis centered on the economic (or class) dimensions of stratification, but Weber believed that the prestige (social honor) and political dimensions of stratification were sometimes independently important. These other dimensions of stratification could change without change in the economic dimension, or they could remain stable despite changes in the economic dimension. With his widely ranging erudition, Weber illustrated

9

his thesis by showing that, for example, a high status group, such as the Prussian Junkers, could retain considerable political power despite its reduced economic importance. Conversely, a rising economic group, such as the bourgeoisie, had to conduct a long struggle to obtain the prestige equivalent to its economic position. Weber did not seek to overturn Marx's analysis but to go beyond it—to broaden its perspectives.[5]

In his analysis of the economic or "class" dimension of stratification, Weber shifted from Marx's focus on the sphere of production to the market or exchange, defining *class* as "a number of people who have in common a specific causal component of their life chances in so far as this component is represented exclusively by economic interest in the possession of goods and opportunities for income, and is represented under the conditions of commodity or labor markets."[6] The economic dimension of stratification, in Weber's conceptualization, included a great variety of explicit and implicit market relationships.

In the twentieth century Weber's notion of class must be widened beyond that of property and the market. In the "welfare state," in particular, many important elements of the command over resources become available as public services.[7] The distribution and quality of these public services affect the absolute and relative well-being of all individuals.[8] Considerable inconsistency *may* exist between the income and basic services of persons or groups.[9] While the two are fairly closely linked in the United States, poor basic services are *not*

10

associated with low income in Sweden. A larger issue is also involved. As Marshall has argued, the welfare-state approach breaks the link between the market and well-being.[10]

Titmuss has further refined our tools of analysis by conceiving of *income* as the "command over resources over time."[11] He argues that wage-connected benefits (for example, pensions) and fiscal benefits (for example, tax deductions for children which benefit the high-income more than the low-income taxpayer), as well as welfare (transfer) benefits, must be included in any discussion of the command over *resources* or living standards. Even this expanded perspective fails to denote all the concerns that we have today in dealing with poverty and inequality. We are concerned also with the individual's political role, his self-respect, and his children's opportunities.

These concerns mean that the role of government is tremendously increased.[12] To a growing extent, the individual's command over resources depends on his relation to government, whether in terms of income tax, subsidies, licensing, or public services.[13] Therefore, as Reich has maintained, the concept of property, must be enlarged and altered to include pension accumulations and rights to governmental largesse and services, especially education. Property, in the more conventional sense, still remains important, but other forms of rights of access and availability are beginning to acquire similar significance.

This broadened view of "the command over re-

11

sources," suggested by Titmuss, Reich, and Marshall, requires us to range beyond the economic. Poverty is not only a condition of economic insufficiency; it is also social and political exclusion. We suggest that *a minimum approach by government in any society with significant inequalities must provide for rising minimum levels, not only of (1) incomes, (2) assets, and (3) basic services, but also of (4) self-respect and (5) opportunities for education and social mobility and (6) participation in many forms of decision-making.*

Our purpose in Part I is to discuss each of these six dimensions of well-being. Two chapters will be devoted to the income dimension and one chapter to each of the other dimensions of inequality. In each chapter we seek to (1) explain the dimension of well-being under consideration, (2) examine existing data on distribution with regard to that dimension, (3) identify the social indicators needed for further analysis, (4) outline the short-term goals of inequality reduction and define minimum levels of well-being, and (5) suggest implications of the data and analysis for social policy.

The movement within the six dimensions of well-being is not always synchronized; movement in one dimension does not necessarily mean that similar movement occurs in other dimensions. For example, although the current income of two families may be the same, the level of living of one may be vastly inferior to that of the other because the families differ in housing conditions.

Analysis of inequality in terms of these six dimensions can aid social scientists in *program planning* by pointing out the diverse and frequently conflicting goals of programs, and by highlighting the relatively neglected aspects of poverty. For example, in planning poverty programs we will wish to ask:

1. At what dimension of inequality is the program aimed, for example, the economic, service, political, educational and social mobility, or status dimensions of stratification?
2. Is the program aimed at placing a floor under the social conditions of those who are poor (that is, minimum levels of jobs, incomes, housing, health, self-respect through guaranteed work with guaranteed minimum wages, Guaranteed Annual Income, Medicaid-Medicare, Social Security, and housing programs) *or* opening the door of opportunity to some of those who are poor so that they may move out of poverty into other niches in society (for example, through educational and job training programs)?

This analysis may also assist in *program evaluation* by providing a framework for pinpointing the goals of the programs in question and for showing the relationships among the goals of various programs—first steps in any assessment.

The six dimensions of well-being lead policy-makers who deal with the poor to ask what kinds of responsibilities and burdens our society should have. Since we do not have the resources to accomplish all our goals within the next ten years, our nation must decide to what extent do we wish to improve neighborhood amenities, legal services, the education of youth, or the health of our senior citizens? To a large extent, these are not narrow technical issues but value issues which may be expected to produce acrimonious debate. Social indicators, such as those discussed in this book, will not tell us what choices to make between growth and inequality reduction, spending money on health services or education, price increases or expansion, and the like. But we hope that these indicators can prevent us from ignoring the fact that we are making choices.

More effective measurements, such as those proposed by supporters of Senator Walter Mondale's Full Opportunity and Social Accounting Act (1967, S.843), will improve our ability to comprehend the kinds of programs that are likely to be useful for a particular purpose. But hopes for compelling evaluations and knowledge are at least premature. We seek new knowledge brought out by social indicators to direct the nation, freshly and more acutely, to the issues of choice that are frequently ignored in a political rhetoric and in a social science that are inadequate in dealing with the subtleties of late-twentieth-century life. Social indicators can arouse groups, outside the government as well as within, to delineate the nature of progress and how well it is being achieved and distributed. In these assessments, low consensus will emerge. The ensuing debates would be concerned with the central issues of a just society. Social indicators would then contribute to useful conflict rather than to evasive complacency.

Our second purpose in this book is to show that stratification theory can be refined and modernized through understanding of poverty action. The bearing that empirical research and theory have upon one another has long been emphasized by Robert Merton and others.[14] Applied social science should also be a "two way street," both drawing from and contributing to social theory. The many recent "applied" analyses of poverty need to be distilled and added to the general corpus of sociological theory.[15] Conceptually, the writings of Titmuss on the distribution of "command over resources" need to be connected with those of Parsons and Marshall on the meaning of citizenship[16] while Max Weber has to be Americanized. The interpretation of any particular historical period may require an expansion of the number of stratificational dimensions or, at least, a recognition of the peculiar and changing content of each dimension.[17] The dimension that is of major importance may also change.[18]

We hope that other social scientists will also attempt to relate applied and theoretical social science. We believe that doing so will enrich American social science by forcing the consideration of generally neglected facts, by pressing for reconsideration of misleading or incorrect theories, by clarifying vague concepts, and by generating new theories or conceptual schemes. We are persuaded, with Dahrendorf, that if we as social scien-

tists " . . . regain the problem-consciousness which has
been lost in the last decades, we cannot fail to recover
the critical engagement in the realities of our social
world which we need to do our job well."[19] We believe
that refinement of stratification theory through analysis
of applied sociology will, in turn, strengthen the efforts
of social scientists to reduce poverty and inequality.

NOTES

1. Stanislaw Ossowski, *Class Structure in the Social Consciousness* (New York: The Free Press, 1963), p. 133.
   A similar point has been made in E. P. Thompson, *The
   Making of the English Working Classes* (New York:
   Vintage Books, 1963).
2. Mollie Orshansky, "How Poverty Is Measured," *Monthly
   Labor Review* (February 1969), p. 38.
3. We will not discuss the inequalities which affect other
   than low-income groups, for example, youth, women,
   and minority groups. We do discuss inequalities affect-
   ing women in S. M. Miller, Pamela Roby, and Daphne
   Joslin, "Social Problems of the Future," in Erwin O.
   Smigel, ed., *Handbook of Social Problems* (Chicago:
   Rand McNally, forthcoming).
4. Max Weber, "Class, Status, Party," in Hans Gerth and
   C. Wright Mills, eds. and trans., *From Max Weber*
   (New York: Oxford University Press, 1958).
5. See "Introduction" in S. M. Miller, ed., *Max Weber:
   Readings* (New York: Thomas Y. Crowell Company,
   1964).

6. Weber, *op. cit.*
7. Many sociologists have observed elements of the development of the break between market and well-being. For example, Parsons has noted that public control of private business contributed to the inclusion of Negroes and other groups, and that government control over the value of the dollar shapes the distribution of wealth. Talcott Parsons, "Full Citizenship for the Negro American? A Sociological Problem," *Daedalus*, XCIV, No. 4 (Fall 1965).
8. Brian Abel-Smith has contested some prevailing views of the distribution of benefits in his trenchant "Whose Welfare State?" in Norman MacKenzie, ed., *Conviction* (London: MacGibbon & Kee, 1958).
9. The Davis and Moore proposition states, in brief, that "social stratification, the uneven distribution of material rewards and prestige, is functionally necessary . . . and inevitable in any society" for it is a source of motivation for individuals to fill positions which are important to society and which require special talents or training. Wesolowski questioned the "inevitability" of an uneven distribution of material rewards by pointing out that in Poland and Norway the range of income has been distinctly narrowed but education and other services have been expanded. In these countries, he contends, not "material rewards" but authority (which gives one the opportunity to express his own personality) and education are viewed as "end values" or sources of motivation. In support of his thesis that occupational prestige is not an important motivational force under the Polish value system, Wesolowski cites Dr. Adam Sarapata's finding that 50 per cent of the respondents in a survey of Lodz

replied "no" when asked if some occupations were more important than others. Wlodzimierz Wesolowski, "Some Notes on the Functional Theory of Stratification," in Reinhard Bendix and Seymour Martin Lipset, *Class, Status, and Power* (New York: The Free Press, 1966).

10. T. H. Marshall, *Class, Citizenship and Social Development* (New York: Doubleday & Company, Inc., 1963), pp. 78–133.

11. Richard M. Titmuss, *Income Distribution and Social Change* (London: G. Allen and Unwin, Ltd., 1962), p. 2 ff; also, *Essays on the Welfare State* (New Haven: Yale University Press, 1959); also "The New Income" in S. M. Miller and Frank Riessman, *Social Class and Social Policy* (New York: Basic Books, Inc., 1968). We frequently refer in the following analysis to the poorest of the poor for we suspect that their conditions are more difficult than the rest of the poor, and their interests by and large are neglected in current discussions of poverty programs. For a discussion of the involvement of the poorest in poverty programs, see S. M. Miller, Pamela Roby, and Alwine A. de Vos van Steenwijk, "Social Policy and the Excluded Man" (stencil), 1968.

12. Ossowski has noted, for instance:

. . . the experiences of recent years incline us to formulate the Marxian conception of social class in the form of a law which establishes a functional dependence: the more closely the social system approximates to the ideal type of a free and competitive capitalist society, the more are the classes determined by their relation to the means of production, and the more are human relationships determined by ownership of the means of production. . . . the majority of American citizens are becoming accustomed to large-scale activities planned by the central authorities. . . . Hence comes the talk about the crisis facing political economics, whose laws were formerly rooted in the basic and inevitable tendencies of human behavior, but which today faces a dilemma caused by the growing influence of the government as a factor which consciously directs the country's economic life. Ossowski, *op. cit.,* p. 185.

13. The importance of government subsidy and licensing has led Charles Reich to speak of "largesse" in his seminal essay, "The New Property," *Yale Law Review,* XCIII (1964).

14. Robert K. Merton, *Social Theory and Social Structure,* revised ed. (New York: The Free Press, 1957), pp. 85–117; Herbert Blumer, "What Is Wrong with Social Theory," *American Sociological Review,* XIX, No. 1 (February 1954), 3–10.

15. Cf. the first essay by Gouldner and the concluding article by Miller in Alvin W. Gouldner and S. M. Miller, eds., *Applied Sociology* (New York: The Free Press, 1965). Other essays by Miller that bear on the issues of application are "Poverty," *Proceedings, Sixth World Congress of Sociology* (1967), and "Social Change and 'The Age of Psychiatry'" (with Frank Reissman) in Miller and Reissman, *op. cit.*

16. Parsons, *op. cit.;* Marshall, *op. cit.*

17. Cf. Weber, *op. cit.,* p. 185.

18. Many American sociologists were misled into believing that post-World War II society was characterized by consensus simply because conflicts centering around the workplace became considerably less violent than in the 1880's or 1930's. Rather than disappearing, conflicts

have shifted from the workplace to ghetto streets where rebellions are aimed at societal and governmental injustices.

19. Ralf Dahrendorf, "Out of Utopia: Toward a Reorientation of Sociological Analysis," *American Journal of Sociology,* LXIV (1958–1959), 115–127.

2
Poverty as Income Deficiency: Three Approaches

Poverty is usually thought of as income deficiency. The argument of the first section of this book is that inequality rather than poverty is the main issue and that the income-deficiency orientation is limited. Succeeding chapters deal with the dimensions of economic, social, and psychological well-being that are neglected in the overriding emphasis on low income alone.

Within the income-deficiency approach, grave disagreements exist about the best way of measuring inadequate incomes. One approach, by far the most widely used, is to define poverty in terms of a cost-of-living budget estimate. This is the "poverty line" emphasis that marks current policy. It purports to define poverty in terms of an "absolute" standard needed to

21

maintain a minimum level of living and therefore does not seem to be about inequality, the relation of the low income to higher income groups. In fact, as we shall see, the standard shifts slowly with the rising expenditure levels of the general population.

The other two approaches to measuring income deficiency are frankly about inequality. The second defines the poverty or low-income or adequacy line as a percentage of mean or median family income in the United States. Changes in average income would automatically change the definition of what it is to have an inadequate income. There is no suggestion that a fixed basket of basic goods for survival is being priced.

The third approach views low income in terms of the share of total national income going to the bottom 10, 20, or 30 per cent of the population. The most frequent concern is with the bottom 20 per cent. This orientation emerges directly from a concern with inequality—how the total economic pie is being cut. In this approach, poverty can no longer be discussed since what is examined is a particular slice of the income distribution over time to see whether there is gain or loss. In the first two approaches, a decline or expansion in the number of poor can be estimated; in the third orientation, this is not possible.

These three approaches of defining well-being—by a budget-oriented poverty line, by comparative income, or by examination of the share of the bottom fifth—not only lead to different estimates of the size (in the case of the first two methods) and direction of "poverty" but also to different characteristics of the poor. The three sets of measurements of income inadequacy define different parts of the American population as having inadequate incomes.

In this chapter we will examine each of these approaches to income measurement. Readers who are not interested in technical comparisons among these three approaches may wish to skip to the conclusion of this chapter.

BUDGET-ORIENTED APPROACHES

Obviously, the line that separates the poor from the nonpoor or the poor from the poorer is not clear-cut.[1] A fundamental issue in delineating the cutoff point between the poor and others is whether poverty is to be considered as barest survival or as inadequacy in terms of prevailing standards. A second issue, which becomes almost technical, is assessing how many gradations and modifications should be made for varying conditions which affect the assessment of need (family size and composition, regional cost differences, and so on).

Within the budget-oriented approaches, wide variations exist in the placement of the poverty line. Obviously, the aim is to provide an "adequate" level of income; immediately the issue then becomes "adequate for what?" An income level that permits a family to survive is one thing; an income level that brings fami-

23

124148

lies closer to prevailing standards is quite another; and an income level that provides a stimulus for social mobility, a great concern of the war on poverty, is probably still another. Where the line is drawn will deeply affect the number and characteristics of those who are defined as poor. In addition, it will as deeply affect the assessment of failure or success in poverty-reduction efforts.

In 1966, Ornati synthesized sixty budgets for workers' families prepared during the twentieth century by governmental and private agencies. His study points out the circularity in the definition of budget criteria between what people ought to have and what people actually do have. It also shows an increase over the years of the relative levels at which the three concepts of minimum subsistence, adequacy, and comfort have been defined.[2]

Similarly the difference between the 1951 and 1966 Bureau of Labor Statistics "City Worker's Family Budget" for a moderate living standard illustrates the changes in educational levels, the cultural developments growing out of travel and migration, and the growth in purchasing power that have affected the level of living of American families and their ideas about what constitutes a moderate living standard. The 1951 "modest but adequate" budget for a city worker's family cost $4,200; in 1966 the comparable "moderate budget" was priced at $8,700. *Sixty per cent of the rise in the standard was due to the upgrading of living standards, rather than to price increases.*[3]

24

Since 1964, the most commonly used and now official set of poverty lines is the one developed by Mollie Orshansky of the Social Security Administration (SSA) of the U.S. Department of Health, Education and Welfare. The Orshansky (SSA) poverty line takes into account family size, composition, farm-nonfarm residence, and proportions of income required to purchase a minimum adequate diet. It satisfied the requirement of political feasibility, for the overall numbers of poor in 1964 did not change from those enumerated by the Council of Economic Advisors which utilized a $3,000 poverty line unadjusted for family size and other characteristics. On the other hand, the characteristics of the poor did change (see Table 2-1). By 1966, 900,000 fewer American families (6.1 million as compared with 7.0 million) had incomes below the SSA level than below the $3,000 income line (see Table 2-2).

Any relative-poverty budget line builds on numerous value assumptions. The SSA poverty line assumes the following: the significance of each additional family member for family budgetary needs; the economic importance of urban or rural residence; the proportion of the family budget allotted to food expenditures; the definition of adequate diet; and the standard of food requirements set by proportion of households at which the achievement of adequate nutrition is defined as tolerable (because of food preferences, even some well-to-do households do not have nutritionally adequate diets).

Despite these value assumptions, the SSA poverty

TABLE 2-1 Social Security Administration's Poverty and Low-Income Criteria[a] for Families of Different Composition, March 1967

Number of Family Members	Poverty Level						Low-Income Level					
	Nonfarm			Farm			Nonfarm			Farm		
	Total	Male head	Female head	Total	Male head	Female head	Total	Male head	Female head	Total	Male head	Female head
1 member	$1,635	$1,710	$1,595	$1,145	$1,180	$1,110	$1,985	$2,080	$1,930	$1,390	$1,440	$1,340
Head under age 65	1,685	1,760	1,625	1,195	1,230	1,140	2,045	2,140	1,975	1,450	1,495	1,380
Head aged 65 or over	1,565	1,580	1,560	1,095	1,105	1,090	1,890	1,925	1,880	1,330	1,350	1,313
2 members	2,115	2,130	2,055	1,475	1,480	1,400	2,855	2,875	2,735	1,990	2,000	1,870
Head under age 65	2,185	2,200	2,105	1,535	1,540	1,465	2,945	2,970	2,790	2,075	2,080	1,945
Head aged 65 or over	1,970	1,975	1,955	1,380	1,380	1,370	2,665	2,675	2,615	1,870	1,875	1,833
3 members	2,600	2,610	2,515	1,815	1,820	1,725	3,425	3,440	3,330	2,400	2,400	2,325
4 members	3,335	3,335	3,320	2,345	2,345	2,320	4,345	4,355	4,255	3,060	3,060	3,000
5 members	3,930	3,930	3,895	2,755	2,755	2,755	5,080	5,085	4,970	3,565	3,565	3,560
6 members	4,410	4,410	4,395	3,090	3,090	3,075	5,700	5,710	5,600	3,995	4,000	3,920
7 or more members	5,430	5,440	5,310	3,790	3,795	3,760	6,945	6,960	6,780	4,850	4,850	4,815

[a]Required income in 1966 according to Social Security Administration poverty or low-income index for a family of a given size and composition. Family income criteria weighted together in accordance with percentage distribution of total units by number of related children and sex of head, as of Current Population Survey, March 1967.
For detailed description of the Social Security Administration measure of poverty and low income and their rationale, see the Social Security Bulletin (January 1965), pp. 3-11, and (July 1965), pp. 3-10.

SOURCE: Mollie Orshansky, "The Shape of Poverty in 1966," Social Security Bulletin (March 1968), Table 1, p. 4.

TABLE 2-2: Families with Incomes under $3,000 and under the SSA Poverty Level in 1966 (numbers in millions)

Characteristic of Family Head	Incomes under $3,000		Income below SSA Poverty Level	
	Number	Per Cent	Number	Per Cent
All heads	7.0	100	6.1	100
Aged, female, or nonwhite head	4.9	71	3.9	64
Head aged 65 and over	2.8	40	1.5	25
Female head	1.9	27	1.8	30
Nonwhite head	1.5	21	1.7	28

SOURCE: Mollie Orshansky, *Research and Statistics Note No. 24* (U.S. Department of Health, Education and Welfare, Social Security Administration, Office of Research and Statistics, December 10, 1968).

line can be considered as only quasi-relative. Between 1959 and 1965, it took into account only the changes in consumer prices; the poverty line has not been adjusted to reflect the increases in the rising level of living enjoyed by the rest of the population. As a consequence, it is woefully inadequate in measuring poverty today.[4]

The SSA poverty line has also been questioned from the other perspective—that it is too high. The SSA estimates assume that the family budget is less than three times the food budget for families of three or more persons and 27 per cent for families of two persons. In contrast, Rose Friedman, who developed a considerably lower poverty line based upon the same "economy" food plan of the Department of Agriculture's National Research Council, argued for the use of a family budget in which three-fourths of the households have two-thirds of the Council's recommended eight nutrients.[5]

In the affluent United States, we must question whether the SSA's income-food relationship is adequate. Both the SSA and Friedman use the "economy" food plan, which was issued by the Department of Agriculture for "temporary or emergency use when funds are low." The SSA's second budget line—the *near-poor*—is based upon the low-cost food plan of the Department of Agriculture, which provided total food expenditures of only 75 cents a day per person (in an average four-person family) in 1966. Spending at this level does not guarantee an adequate diet. As Orshansky points out, families spending less are certainly more likely to have diets falling below the recommended allowances for important nutrients.

The basic assumptions of the economy and the low-cost food plans are questionable. First, both assume that all meals are prepared at home from foods that are purchased at retail. Since eating out has become an American norm, this assumption may be seriously misleading. The second assumption is that families will, or even can, spend their food money to buy the most nutritious foods.[6] The poor, are generally not buyer-wise and are often unable to spend time comparative shopping. Consequently, they have difficulty obtaining food at the retail prices suggested by the Department of Agriculture.

Many issues are involved in the question of whether

28

the SSA budget or any other budget for that matter is adequate. An increase in the SSA budget would increase strikingly the number of poor. We believe that poverty lines based upon budget-oriented approaches will continue to be inadequate because of the deep political implications involved in each upward adjustment. Frequently, as occurred in the late 1960's, a budget-based poverty line that is rapidly falling further behind the rising standard of living enjoyed by the rest of the population will not be adjusted upward until that change appears politically feasible.[7] For this practical reason as well as for conceptual reasons, we believe that in the United States it is more appropriate to view income deficiency clearly in terms of inequality by utilizing the comparative approach to poverty (for instance, to define families as suffering from income poverty if they are below one-half of the nation's median income), or the income share approach of analyzing changes in the percentage of total national income going to those in the lower end of the income distribution.[8] In these ways, the criteria used in delineating the poor would automatically shift upward with the rising level of living in the economy and would be more independent of political issues.

CHARACTERISTICS OF THE POOR:
THE SSA INDEX AND THE $3,000 LINE

The mode of estimating the poor—even within the budget-oriented approach—affects the characteristics

29

of the poor and shifts the focus of the problem of poverty.

In 1966, 6.1 million American families had incomes below the Social Security Administration poverty level, and 7.0 million families were below the $3,000 income line. The incidence of poverty among different groups also varied according to the two poverty lines. In 1966, Orshansky reported that seven out of ten families with incomes of less than $3,000 fell in one of three categories—aged, nonwhite, or female head—compared with two out of three families classed as poor by the Social Security Administration index (see Table 2–2).

Table 2–3 shows the incidence of poverty according to SSA criteria among various categories of families and unrelated individuals in 1966. Orshansky summarizes the demographic characteristics of the poor as follows:

Minorities, however defined, were less favored than the rest. Counted (among the 45 million Americans designated as poor in 1965) were nearly one in four of those living on farms, compared with one in seven of the nonfarm population, but most of the poor were not on a farm. The total with low incomes included from 12 to 19 per cent of the white population and from 41 to 54 per cent of the nonwhite. Of the total in poverty, however, two out of three were white, and among the near poor, four out of five were white.[9]

About half of all the Nation's poor families—one-seventh of the white poor and two-thirds of the nonwhite poor— lived in the South in 1966 . . . Despite the exodus of many nonwhite persons from the South in recent years, the South (was) still home for about half of all nonwhite families in the country . . . In 1966, white families in the South on an average had only $5 in income for every $6 enjoyed by white families elsewhere; Southern nonwhite families averaged less than $3 for every $5 of income of nonwhite families outside the South.[10]

Although the number of Americans below the SSA poverty level dropped from 38.9 million in 1959 to 29.65 million in 1966, the number termed *near poor* by the SSA—those with incomes barely above the poverty threshold—decreased by only 0.6 million (from 15.8 to 15.2 million) during the seven-year period. In addition, Orshansky points out: ". . . another 5 million would be added to the ranks of the economically deprived were we to include the 2 million persons in institutions —not now in the count but ranking among the poorest of the poor—as well as the many aged persons and parent-child groups not now on the poverty roll but who would be there if they had to rely on their own resources instead of on those of the more fortunate relatives whose homes they share."[11]

The total difference between the actual incomes of persons classified as below the SSA poverty line and the incomes which would be required for them to be classified as nonpoor (although still near-poor) was $11 billion in 1965, $2.7 billion less than in 1959.[12]

Among the nation's poor many persons could do little on their own to improve their incomes. Either they were unable to work, or they were poor despite the fact that they worked full-time throughout the year.

31

TABLE 2-3 The Poor and Near Poor: Persons in Households and Unrelated Individuals below SSA Poverty Level and above That Level but below Low-Income Level by Family Status, Sex, Race, and Other Specific Characteristics, 1966 (numbers in thousands)

Persons in Households

Family Status	Total	All households Poor Number	All households Poor Per Cent	All households Near poor Number	All households Near poor Per Cent	With male head Total	With male head Poor Number	With male head Poor Per Cent	With male head Near poor Number	With male head Near poor Per Cent	With female head Total	With female head Poor Number	With female head Poor Per Cent	With female head Near poor Number	With female head Near poor Per Cent
Total households															
All persons	193,415	29,657	15.3	15,150	7.8	168,536	18,952	11.2	13,031	7.7	24,878	10,704	43.0	2,119	8.5
In families	181,048	24,836	13.7	14,369	7.9	163,972	17,675	10.8	12,750	7.8	17,075	7,160	41.9	1,619	9.5
Head	49,922	6,086	12.4	3,554	7.3	43,750	4,276	9.8	3,061	7.0	5,171	1,810	35.0	492	9.5
Children under age 18	69,771	12,539	18.0	6,637	9.5	62,521	8,117	13.0	5,932	9.5	7,251	4,423	61.0	705	9.7
Other family members	62,355	6,211	10.0	4,178	6.7	57,701	5,282	9.2	3,757	6.5	4,653	927	19.9	422	9.1
Unrelated individuals	12,367	4,821	39.0	781	6.3	4,564	1,277	28.0	281	6.2	7,803	3,544	45.4	500	6.4
Under age 65	7,489	2,124	28.4	312	4.2	3,279	712	21.7	146	4.5	4,210	1,412	33.5	166	3.9
Aged 65 and over	4,878	2,697	55.3	469	9.6	1,285	565	44.0	135	10.5	3,593	2,132	59.3	334	9.3
White households															
All persons	170,384	20,313	11.9	12,278	7.2	151,265	13,417	8.9	10,651	7.0	19,120	6,896	36.1	1,627	8.5
In families	159,598	16,287	10.2	11,601	7.3	147,445	12,410	8.4	10,427	7.1	12,154	3,877	31.9	1,174	9.7
Head	44,016	4,375	9.9	2,968	6.7	40,006	3,264	8.2	2,586	6.5	4,010	1,111	27.7	382	9.5
Children under age 18	59,578	7,526	12.6	5,222	8.8	55,103	5,280	9.6	4,732	8.6	4,475	2,246	50.2	492	11.0
Other family members	56,004	4,386	7.8	3,411	6.1	52,336	3,866	7.4	3,109	5.9	3,669	521	14.2	300	8.2
Unrelated individuals	10,786	4,026	37.3	677	6.3	3,820	1,007	26.4	224	5.9	6,966	3,019	43.3	453	6.5
Under age 65	6,296	1,626	25.8	241	3.8	2,688	540	20.1	110	4.1	3,608	1,086	30.1	131	3.6
Aged 65 and over	4,490	2,400	53.5	436	9.7	1,132	467	41.3	114	10.1	3,358	1,933	57.6	322	9.6
Nonwhite households															
All persons	23,034	9,345	40.6	2,873	12.5	17,271	5,535	32.0	2,381	13.8	5,761	3,809	66.1	492	8.5
In families	21,450	8,549	39.9	2,768	12.9	16,527	5,265	31.9	2,323	14.1	4,921	3,283	66.7	445	9.0
Head	4,905	1,711	34.9	586	11.9	3,744	1,012	27.0	476	12.7	1,161	699	60.2	111	9.6
Children under age 18	10,193	5,014	49.2	1,413	13.9	7,419	2,837	38.2	1,201	16.2	2,776	2,177	78.4	213	7.7
Other family members	6,352	1,824	28.7	769	12.1	5,364	1,416	26.4	646	12.0	984	407	41.4	121	12.3
Unrelated individuals	1,584	796	50.3	105	6.6	744	270	36.3	58	7.8	840	526	62.6	47	5.6
Under age 65	1,196	499	41.7	72	6.0	592	172	29.1	37	6.3	604	327	54.1	35	5.8
Aged 65 and over	388	297	76.5	33	8.5	152	98	64.5	21	13.8	236	199	84.3	12	5.1

TABLE 2-3 (continued)

Unrelated Individuals

	All unrelated individuals				Male unrelated individuals				Female unrelated individuals			
		Poor				Poor				Poor		
Characteristic	Total	Num-ber	Per Cent	Percent-age distri-bution	Total	Num-ber	Per Cent	Percent-age distri-bution	Total	Num-ber	Per Cent	Percent-age distri-bution
					Total individuals							
Total	12,368	4,820	39.0	100.0	4,563	1,276	28.0	100.0	7,804	3,544	45.4	100.0
Residence:												
Nonfarm	12,068	4,683	38.8	97.2	4,414	1,212	27.5	95.0	7,654	3,471	45.3	97.9
Farm	300	138	46.0	2.9	150	65	43.3	5.1	150	73	48.7	2.1
Region:												
Northeast	3,210	1,172	36.5	24.3	1,136	302	26.6	23.7	2,074	870	41.9	24.5
North Central	3,402	1,362	40.0	28.3	1,173	322	27.5	25.2	2,230	1,039	46.6	29.3
South	3,368	1,573	46.7	32.6	1,257	434	34.5	34.0	2,111	1,139	54.0	32.1
West	2,385	713	29.9	14.8	996	217	21.8	17.0	1,390	496	35.7	14.0
Race:												
White	10,784	4,026	37.3	83.5	3,819	1,007	26.4	78.9	6,965	3,019	43.3	85.2
Nonwhite	1,583	794	50.2	16.5	744	269	36.2	21.1	839	525	62.6	14.8
Age:												
14-24	1,294	509	39.3	10.6	586	194	33.1	15.2	707	314	44.4	8.9
25-34	1,134	159	14.0	3.3	690	69	10.0	5.4	444	89	20.0	2.5
35-44	1,077	220	20.4	4.6	613	81	13.2	6.3	464	139	30.0	3.9
45-54	1,482	364	24.6	7.6	639	127	19.9	10.0	843	237	28.1	6.7
55-64	2,502	872	34.9	18.1	751	238	31.7	18.7	1,752	634	36.2	17.9
65 and over	4,878	2,697	55.3	56.0	1,284	564	43.9	44.2	3,594	2,132	59.3	60.2
Sex:												
Male	4,563	1,276	28.0	26.5	4,563	1,276	28.0	100.0	.....	.....	.....	.....
Female	7,804	3,544	45.4	73.5	.....	.....	.....	.....	7,804	3,544	45.4	100.0
Earner status:												
Earner	7,370	1,459	19.8	30.3	3,335	545	16.3	42.7	4,035	914	22.7	25.8
Nonearner	4,998	3,361	67.2	69.7	1,228	731	59.5	57.3	3,769	2,630	69.8	74.2
Employment status and occupation:												
Employed, March 1967	6,479	1,225	18.9	25.4	2,899	442	14.6	33.1	3,580	804	22.5	22.7
Professional and technical workers	1,294	192	14.8	4.0	559	60	10.7	4.7	735	133	18.1	3.8
Farmers and farm managers	102	31	30.4	.6	82	25	(1)	2.0	21	6	(1)	.2
Managers, officials, and proprietors (except farm)	507	50	9.9	1.0	306	20	6.5	1.6	201	31	15.4	.9
Clerical and sales workers	1,567	155	9.9	3.2	385	43	11.2	3.4	1,180	111	9.4	3.1
Craftsmen and fore-men	431	38	8.8	.8	382	29	7.6	2.3	49	9	(1)	.3
Operatives	889	97	10.9	2.0	505	41	8.1	3.2	384	55	14.3	1.6
Service workers	1,361	545	40.0	11.3	360	86	23.9	6.7	1,002	459	45.8	13.0
Private household workers	425	288	67.8	6.0	7	7	(1)	.5	419	281	67.1	7.9
Laborers (except mine)	328	117	35.7	2.4	320	118	36.9	9.2	8	.....	.....	.....
Unemployed	287	103	35.9	2.1	176	60	34.1	4.7	112	42	37.5	1.2
Not in labor force	5,603	3,492	62.3	72.4	1,491	794	53.3	62.2	4,113	2,697	65.8	76.1

SOURCE: Derived by the Social Security Administration from special tabulations by the Bureau of the Census from the Current Population Survey for March 1967. Mollie Orshansky, "The Shape of Poverty in 1966," *Social Security Bulletin* (March 1968), pp. 5,8.

In 1966 among the 45 million Americans whose incomes fell below the poverty or near poverty level were 18 to 28 per cent of the nation's children and from 30 to 43 per cent of the aged; 25 per cent of all poor families (including 8 million persons) were headed by a man who worked throughout the year.[13]

COMPARATIVE INCOME

What is the scope and character of poverty in a comparative approach? In this procedure, median or mean family income for the United States is taken as the standard; the poverty line is 50 per cent of the standard, and the line for the poorest of the poor may be 33 or 25 per cent of the standard.[14] This approach openly embraces the notion that the condition of poverty is an inequality phenomenon—the poor are those who have fallen behind the grades and standards of the society as a whole, as Galbraith states.[15]

Using the standard of 50 per cent of median family income, the poverty line was $2,774 in 1960.[16] In that year 20 per cent of the nation's families were living below this level; that is, they were "in poverty." This contrasts with Orshansky's figure for 1960, which showed 24 per cent of households in poverty, and converges with the statistics of the Council of Economic Advisors, which found that 20 per cent of the country's families had incomes below $3,000 (1962 prices) in 1960.[17]

The trend data are particularly striking, for *the median income standard shows that the percentage of poor has not declined since 1947.* Between 1947 and 1965, as shown in Table 2–2, although families with incomes less than $3,000 (1965 prices) declined from 30.9 to 16.5 per cent, families with incomes of less than one-half the median increased from 18.9 to 20.0 per cent (see Table 2–4). In 1959, the median income for four-person families was $6,070, about twice the SSA poverty line; in 1966, the median income for four-person families was $8,340—two and one-half times the SSA nonfarm poverty threshold of $3,335. In other words, Orshansky notes, the average income of four-person families increased by 37 per cent, but the SSA poverty line (adjusted only for price increases) increased by only 9 per cent, or one-fourth as much.[18] In the 1960's, unlike earlier periods, the budget-oriented estimates have not changed to keep up with changes in average styles of life. This break with previous practice is because of political, not conceptual, constraints.

POVERTY AS INCOME SHARE

A third way of looking at the income component of poverty is in terms of the share of the total national income that goes to the bottom 10, 20, or 30 per cent of the population. In this approach, poverty is sharply regarded as inequality. It is the income fate of a specific group which is at the bottom of society that

TABLE 2-4: Percentage of U.S. Families Classified as Poor by Relative and Absolute Standards, 1947-1965

Year	Median income (1965 dollars)	Percentage of Families with Income		
		Less than one-half the median[a]	Less than $3,000 (1965 prices)	Less than $2,000 (1965 prices)
1947	$4,275	18.9	30.0	17.2
1948	4,198	19.1	31.2	18.1
1949	4,116	20.2	32.3	19.5
1950	4,351	20.0	29.9	18.1
1951	4,507	18.9	27.8	16.3
1952	4,625	18.9	26.3	15.8
1953	5,002	19.8	24.6	15.4
1954	4,889	20.9	26.2	16.7
1955	5,223	20.0	23.6	14.6
1956	5,561	19.6	21.5	13.0
1957	5,554	19.7	21.7	13.0
1958	5,543	19.8	21.8	12.8
1959	5,856	20.0	20.6	12.1
1960	5,991	20.3	20.3	12.1
1961	6,054	20.3	20.1	11.9
1962	6,220	19.8	18.9	10.9
1963	6,440	19.9	18.0	10.2
1964	6,676	19.9	17.1	9.2
1965	6,882	20.0	16.5	9.1

[a]Estimated by interpolation.

SOURCE: Victor R. Fuchs, "Redefining Poverty and Redistributing Income," *The Public Interest*, VIII (Summer 1967), 90.

is the issue. Obviously, from this perspective, we cannot have trends in the number and percentage of poor. The question instead is: How well is the bottom group doing? (Some critics of poverty efforts have not always understood that talking about poverty as income share prevents talking about trends in the extent of poverty.)

The discouraging report, as shown in Table 2–5, is that the percentage of total money income that goes to the bottom 20 per cent of families has hovered around 5 per cent since 1947.[19] No great progress has been made in increasing the share of the bottom 20 per cent, despite the widely heralded decline in the share of the top 5 per cent.[20] The total money income that goes to the lowest quintile of families rose only 0.3 per cent between 1947 and 1967, from 5.1 to 5.4 per cent. Over the years, the share of income held by the bottom quintile of individuals hovered around 3.0 per cent. The reduction in the concentration of income at the top has not benefited those at the bottom. *"The Income Revolution," touted in the 1950's as the graceful succumbing of inequality to economic growth, has not occurred.*

CHARACTERISTICS OF PERSONS IN
THE BOTTOM INCOME QUINTILE

Which families are most likely to be at the bottom rungs of the nation's income distribution? The University of Michigan's Survey Research Center's reports on

TABLE 2-5: Distribution of Total Money Income Received by Each Fifth and the Top 5 Per Cent of Families and Unrelated Individuals, 1947 to 1967 (total money income)

Family Income (percentages)

Year	Total	Lowest fifth	Second fifth	Middle fifth	Fourth fifth	Highest fifth	Top 5
1967	100.0	5.4	12.2	17.5	23.7	41.2	15.3
1966	100.0	5.5	12.4	17.7	23.7	40.7	14.8
1965	100.0	5.3	12.1	17.7	23.7	41.3	15.8
1964	100.0	5.2	12.0	17.6	24.0	41.1	15.4
1963	100.0	5.1	12.1	17.6	23.6	41.6	15.8
1962	100.0	5.1	12.0	17.3	23.8	41.7	16.3
1961	100.0	4.8	11.7	17.4	23.6	42.5	17.2
1960	100.0	4.9	12.0	17.7	23.4	42.1	16.9
1959	100.0	5.1	12.1	17.8	23.6	41.4	16.3
1958	100.0	5.1	12.4	17.8	23.7	41.0	15.8
1957	100.0	5.0	12.6	18.1	23.7	40.5	15.8
1956	100.0	4.9	12.4	17.9	23.6	41.1	16.4
1955	100.0	4.8	12.2	17.7	23.4	41.8	16.8
1954	100.0	4.5	12.0	17.6	24.0	41.9	16.4
1953	100.0	4.7	12.4	17.8	24.0	41.0	15.8
1952	100.0	4.9	12.2	17.1	23.5	42.2	17.7
1951	100.0	4.9	12.5	17.6	23.3	41.8	16.9
1950	100.0	4.5	11.9	17.4	23.6	42.7	17.3
1949	100.0	4.5	11.9	17.3	23.5	42.8	16.9
1948	100.0	5.0	12.1	17.2	23.2	42.5	17.1
1947	100.0	5.1	11.8	16.7	23.2	43.3	17.5

TABLE 2-5 (continued)

Unrelated Individual Income (percentages)

Year	Total	Lowest fifth	Second fifth	Middle fifth	Fourth fifth	Highest fifth	Top 5
1967	100.0	3.0	7.5	13.3	24.4	51.8	22.0
1966	100.0	2.8	7.5	13.2	23.8	52.7	22.5
1965	100.0	2.6	7.6	13.5	25.1	51.2	20.2
1964	100.0	2.6	7.0	12.9	24.3	53.2	22.5
1963	100.0	2.6	7.2	12.5	24.6	53.0	21.2
1962	100.0	3.3	7.3	12.5	24.1	52.8	21.3
1961	100.0	2.9	6.8	12.8	24.2	53.3	22.6
1960	100.0	3.0	7.0	13.3	25.7	51.0	20.3
1959	100.0	2.5	6.9	12.8	23.9	53.8	23.2
1958	100.0	2.6	7.0	13.0	24.9	52.5	21.4
1957	100.0	2.9	7.2	13.6	25.3	51.0	19.7
1956	100.0	2.9	6.9	13.7	25.3	51.3	20.4
1955	100.0	2.4	7.3	13.4	24.8	52.0	21.9
1954	100.0	2.5	7.2	12.7	24.5	53.0	22.8
1953	100.0	2.3	6.8	13.5	24.4	53.0	25.3
1952	100.0	2.5	7.5	14.7	25.4	50.0	20.8
1951	100.0	2.9	7.0	14.1	26.7	49.4	18.2
1950	100.0	3.1	6.9	13.1	26.6	50.3	19.3
1949	100.0	3.2	7.4	13.4	25.9	50.2	19.4
1948	100.0	3.3	7.5	13.4	24.9	50.9	20.6
1947	100.0	2.9	5.4	11.5	21.3	58.9	33.3

SOURCE: U.S. Bureau of the Census, *Trends in the Income of Families and Persons in the United States: 1947-1964*, Technical Paper No. 17 by Mary F. Henson (Washington, D.C.: U.S. Government Printing Office, 1967), pp. 176-181; data for years 1965-1967 from U.S. Bureau of the Census, *Current Population Reports*, Series P-60, No. 59, April 13, 1969, Table 25, p. 24.

consumer finances show that in 1964, 42 per cent of the South, as compared with 24 or 25 per cent of other regions, had aggregate family incomes falling within the nation's bottom three income deciles.[21] Of the aged (persons sixty-five years old and over), 28 per cent fell within the lowest deciles and two-thirds within the lowest three deciles of the nation's income distribution. Twenty-four per cent of nonwhite families, as compared with 9 per cent of white families, had incomes falling within the bottom decile, and 58 per cent of nonwhite families, in contrast to 27 per cent of white families, fell within the bottom 30 per cent of the nation's income distribution.[22]

After examining the *incidence* of lagging incomes among various population aggregates, we are led to ask what is the *composition* of the lowest quintile of the population ranked by share of national income? What shifts have occurred in this group which had incomes less than $1,584 in 1947 (in 1964 dollars) and less than $3,288 in 1964?[23]

Between 1947 and 1964, the portion of the bottom quintile which was nonwhite remained fairly constant, hovering around 21 per cent—over twice the portion of nonwhites in the total population. The portion of the lowest fifth residing in each of the four regions also remained fairly constant over the years. Throughout the years, a greater portion of the bottom fifth than of the total population resided in the South (44 per cent of the bottom fifth as compared with 30 per cent of the total population in 1964).

Between 1947 and 1964, the percentage of families in the bottom fifth which were headed by a female increased from 18 to 24 per cent, while the portion of female-headed families in the total population remained constant, around 10 per cent.

The bottom fifth also differed from the total population in terms of the greater portion headed by persons over sixty-five years of age (34 as compared with 14 per cent), the greater portion with no children, and the greater portion not in the labor force (48 as compared with 18 per cent) or employed as farmers, farm managers, private household workers, service workers, farm laborers, and laborers.

The most marked shifts which occurred in the bottom fifth between 1947 and 1964 were the increased proportion of the aged and of clerical, operative, and service workers, and the decreased proportion of farmers or farm managers.[24]

Conclusions: Perspectives on Income Lines

Is there one best way of measuring the extent and trends in income deficiency? Can these three approaches be reduced to one? It is doubtful. In part this is because, as we have found in this chapter, measurement of social problems involves values. The choice of measures or social indicators involves political as well as technical issues. Different interest groups prefer various ways of thinking about poverty: those concerned with economic growth in the context of price stability move toward definitions of poverty along a compressed-budget approach; civil rights groups focus on the income share that goes to blacks. Behind these different orientations and stresses is the uncertainty about what poverty means in an affluent society.

In a surprising reversal, statisticians have anticipated politicians in recognizing the value issues involved in the choice of measurements. Herman P. Miller, Chief of the Population Division of the U.S. Bureau of the Census, pointed out:

Nearly every report on poverty issued by the Federal Government contains the direct or implicit caveat that poverty is relative and that any absolute standard loses its meaning and validity over time. The issue was well stated in the Economic Report of the President last year: "As average incomes rise, society amends its assessment of basic needs. Individuals who cannot afford more than a small fraction of the items enjoyed by the majority are likely to feel deprived. Consequently, an absolute standard that seems appropriate today will inevitably be rejected tomorrow, just as we now reject poverty definitions appropriate a century ago."

Yet, during the past decade we have been measuring poverty by an absolute standard based on relationships that existed in 1955. . . . If we continue to use this definition long enough, we will, in time, eliminate poverty statistically, but few people will believe it—certainly not those who continue to have housing, education, medical care and other goods and services which are far below standards deemed acceptable for this society. . . .

Although there are good reasons for keeping the present definition of poverty, there are even better reasons for changing it. Such a change would undoubtedly create new problems of interpretation and possibly confusion among the public. It makes more sense, however, to accept such risks than to proceed with a definition that increasingly loses touch with reality. With each passing year, the gap between the number of poor obtained by the present definition of poverty and by a reasonable alternative definition will increase, if we continue to have the economic growth that we have enjoyed in the past.[25]

We agree that budget-oriented approaches are inadequate. The better ones, like Orshansky's, sneak in relative issues under the guise of absolute standards. Since our outlook is to avoid ambiguity, and since we believe that over the long run, forthright discussion of issues best meets the needs of the underclass, we advocate clear-cut presentation of poverty data in terms of inequality.

The inequality emphasis leads to a concern with the bottom 20 per cent of the population generally and the bottom 10 per cent particularly. And some would now argue the bottom 50 per cent which includes the neglected and disadvantaged working and middle class groups.[26] It may be difficult to be concerned about the plight of persons within the bottom 20 per cent of society in the United States when their incomes would make them well off in many other societies. While we should not blind ourselves to the magnitude and severity of poverty in other nations, we should not thereby minimize the extent of the poverty problem in our midst.

NOTES

1. In studying the trends shown by estimates of poverty, it is important to be aware of numerical as well as percentage changes over time, for the two may not necessarily move together. Large percentage declines in poverty often blind us to the absolute numbers who remain in that condition. This effect is well illustrated by the significant decline in the percentage of low-income consumer units between 1947 and 1962. Although the percentage decline in families with incomes of under $2,000 between 1947 and 1962 was rather impressive—from 16 to 12 per cent—the actual number of families with incomes under $2,000 declined only minutely, from 7.2 to 7.1 million. Meanwhile, the number of consumer units with incomes of $10,000 and over increased by more than two and one-half times from 4.1 to 10.9 million. Similarly, between 1959 and 1964, the households of poor unrelated persons sixty-five years of age and over declined by 8.8 per cent but numerically increased from 2.5 to 2.8 million. *The Economic Report of the President, 1966,* p. 112. We do not wish to ignore percentage changes, but we do believe that we should be sensitive to the actual number of individual persons who are represented by our statistics.

   The composition of numerical changes in poverty trends should also be given careful attention. The

Economic Report of the President, 1965 showed that the number of poor families declined by 0.3 million—from 9.3 to 9.0 million—between 1962 and 1963 (see the following table). When we adjust for the number of poor families formed and dissolved during this period (0.6 million dissolved; 0.4 million formed), we find that not 0.3 million, but 0.1 million more intact families climbed above the CEA $3,000 poverty line than fell below it. *The Economic Report of the President, 1965,* p. 165.

Changes in Poverty, 1962–1963

Poverty Status of Family	Estimated Number of Poor Families (millions)
Poor families in 1962	9.3
Less. Families no longer poor in 1963	1.8
Poor families dissolved in 1963	0.6
Equals: Families poor in 1962 and 1963	6.9
Plus: Families who became poor in 1963	1.7
Newly formed poor families in 1963	0.4
Equals: Poor families in 1963[a]	9.0

[a] Families with total money income of less than $3,000 (1962 prices).

NOTE: Data relate to families and exclude unrelated individuals. Poor families are defined as all families with total money income of less than $3,000.

The characteristics of the poor vary by the criteria used. As Smolensky noted, between 1947 and 1960 there

45

was a 3.1 percentage point increase in the proportion of poor nonwhite families, using $3,000 (1959 prices) as the definition of poverty, but the proportion of non-whites in the bottom fifth of the population was virtually unchanged between 1947 and 1960. Eugene Smolensky, "The Past and Present Poor," in The Task Force on Economic Growth and Opportunity, U.S. Chamber of Commerce, *The Concept of Poverty* (Washington, D.C.: Government Printing Office, 1965), p. 52.

2. Oscar Ornati, *Poverty Amid Affluence* (New York: The Twentieth Century Fund, 1966).

3. Included in the "upgrading" of the living standards were the following changes: The 1966 food component was based on the U.S. Department of Agriculture's moderate-cost food plan, rather than on an average of the low- and moderate-cost plans which was used previously. (It had been found that although families can achieve nutritional adequacy from the low-cost food plan, only 23 per cent of those who spend amounts equivalent to the cost of this plan actually have nutritionally adequate diets. For the food included in the plan requires a considerable amount of time and skill to prepare.) The 1966 food component also allowed 261 meals away from home, compared with 189 in the original budget. In 1966 the rental component of the housing budget was based on the average of the middle third of the distribution of autumn, 1966 contract rents for units that met the budget criteria of adequacy, and in 1959 it was based on the average rents for *all* units meeting the adequacy criteria. More significantly, the 1966 budget included home-ownership costs for three-fourths of the families for the first time; the 1966 budget

also reflected the increased ownership and use of automobiles accompanying the trend in home ownership and the growth of suburbs without public transportation. The budget also reflected numerous trends in clothing consumption and other personal items. U.S. Department of Labor, Bureau of Labor Statistics, *City Worker's Family Budget,* Bulletin No. 1570–1 (Autumn 1966). In 1967 the Bureau of Labor Statistics developed "low" ($6,021) and "high" in addition to "moderate" ($9,977) budget standards of living for an urban family of four persons. U.S. Department of Labor, Bureau of Labor Statistics, *Three Standards of Living for an Urban Family of Four Persons,* Bulletin No. 1570–5 (Washington, D.C.: U.S. Government Printing Office, 1969). For an analysis of the relationship over time between actual levels of living in the United States and the goals or standards of living which have been accepted in different historical periods and for different purposes, see Helen H. Lamale, "Changes in Concepts of Income Adequacy over the Last Century," *American Economic Review,* LXXVIII (1958), 291–99.

4. Mollie Orshansky, "Counting the Poor: Another Look at the Poverty Profile," *Social Security Bulletin* (July 1965), p. 9.

5. Rose D. Friedman, *Poverty: Definition and Perspective* (Washington, D.C.: American Enterprise Institute, 1966), Table 5, p. 37.

6. David Caplovitz, *The Poor Pay More* (New York: The Free Press, 1963).

7. Poverty estimates based on family-budget lines lead to the comforting conclusion that poverty is disappearing. Thus, *The Economic Report of the President, 1964*

gained popular political support by presenting figures showing the declining number of families with incomes under $3,000 (the CEA's old and well-known poverty line) and under $2,000 in 1962 prices. Families with incomes under $3,000 fell from 32 per cent of the population in 1947 to 19 per cent in 1962. Similarly, the Office of Business Economics showed that the number of consumer units with personal incomes under $3,000 (1959 prices) declined from 59 per cent in 1929 to 24 per cent in 1962.

8. Of course, in countries in which a large proportion of the population is living at or beneath a minimum subsistence level, the comparative or income share approaches would be inadequate.

9. Mollie Orshansky, "The Shape of Poverty in 1966," *Social Security Bulletin* (March 1968), p. 4.

10. Mollie Orshansky, "Counting the Poor: Before and After Federal Income-Support Programs," *Old-Age Income Assurance, Part II: The Aged Population and Retirement Income Programs,* Joint Economic Committee (December 1967), p. 189.

11. Orshansky, "The Shape of Poverty in 1966," p. 4.

12. *Ibid.,* p. 23, Table 12.

13. *Ibid.,* p. 4; and Orshansky, "Counting the Poor: Before and After Federal Income-Support Programs," p. 211.

14. The median is the point which breaks a distribution in half: 50 per cent of the population is above that point, and 50 per cent is below. The mean is the conventional average; all incomes are totaled and then divided by the number of incomes. Owing to the extremely high incomes of a small percentage of families, mean income is considerably higher than median income. In 1962 the

mean family income was $8,151; the median family income was $5,747.

15. John K. Galbraith, *The Affluent Society* (Boston: Houghton Mifflin Company, 1958).

16. Victor Fuchs, "Toward a Theory of Poverty," in Task Force on Economic Growth and Opportunity, *The Concept of Poverty* (Washington, D.C.: U.S. Chamber of Commerce, 1965), p. 75. Median income data were estimated by interpolation.

17. In 1965, 19 per cent of all households (families and unrelated individuals) were poor according to the Social Security Administration's poverty-income standard. *The Annual Report of the Council of Economic Advisors* (Washington, D.C.: U.S. Government Printing Office, 1967), p. 140.

18. Orshansky, "The Shape of Poverty in 1966," p. 6.

19. The decline in the per cent of income held by the bottom quintile of unrelated individuals may be accounted for by the changing composition of households. A much greater percentage of aged poor live alone now than ten years ago. This change increases the percentage of low-income households.

20. A technical aside: Economic statisticians, despite their inventiveness, have failed to innovate new measures of income inequality. The Gini coefficient, the most popular tool for estimating inequality in an income distribution, is not sensitive to the question of what points in the distribution most suffer from inequality. New measures of inequality are needed for the more complicated concerns of today. One example is top-bottom ratios, which compare the share of the top income group (for instance, the upper tenth) with the share of

49

the bottom group. Cf. Harry T. Oshima, "The International Comparison of Size Distribution of Family Incomes with Special Reference to Asia," *Review of Economics and Statistics,* XLIV, No. 4 (November 1962).

21. The Southern poor comprise 45 per cent of all United States poor or near-poor families. Mollie Orshansky, "More About the Poor in 1964," *Social Security Bulletin* (May 1966), pp. 5–7; also, Survey Research Center, University of Michigan, *1965 Survey of Consumer Finances* (Ann Arbor, Mich.: University of Michigan Press, 1966), Tables 1–5, p. 19.

22. Survey Research Center, University of Michigan, *op. cit.,* Tables 1–5, p. 19.

23. U.S. Bureau of the Census, *Trends in the Income of Families and Persons in the United States: 1947–1964,* Technical Paper No. 17 by Mary F. Henson (Washington, D.C.: U.S. Government Printing Office, 1967), p. 188, Tables A, B, C. For further analysis of the distribution of income in the United States see Pamela Roby, "Inequality: A Trend Analysis," *The Annals of the American Academy of Political and Social Science,* CCCLXXXIV (September 1969).

24. In 1966, 37 per cent of the family heads of the bottom fifth as compared with 25 per cent of the SSA poor were over sixty-five, 25 per cent as compared with 30 per cent were female, and 21 per cent as compared with 28 per cent were nonwhite. Mollie Orshansky, *Research and Statistics Note No. 24* (U.S. Department of Health, Education and Welfare, Social Security Administration, Office of Research and Statistics, December 10, 1965); Ida C. Merriam, "Welfare and Its Measurement," in

E. B. Sheldon and Wilbert Moore, eds., *Indicators of Social Change* (New York: Russell Sage Foundation, 1968).

25. Herman P. Miller, "What Is Poverty: Measurement, Profile, Trends," press release for National Industrial Conference Board.

26. S. M. Miller, "Sharing the Burden of Change," *New Generation* (Spring 1969); Brendan Sexton, " 'Middle Class' Workers and the New Politics," *Dissent* (May 1969).

3

Income:
Forms, Stability,
and Goals

Direct annual money income, the subject of the preceding chapter, reflects inadequately the flow of economic benefits to the family. This chapter and the
following one discuss other aspects of economic well-
being. Fringe benefits and the stability of income are
the focus of this chapter; the following chapter con-
centrates on family wealth or assets. Closing the inequality gap requires not only increasing the income of
the poor but improving fringe benefits and security.

FRINGE BENEFITS: NONINCOME COMPENSATION

Fringe benefits, ranging from sandwich lunches for
household domestics to corporate employees' stock
options (which occasionally constitute a greater portion

of executives' compensation than their actual income), quietly but significantly stretch many individuals' "command over resources."[1] These sources of nonmonetary compensation increase the inequalities between poor unorganized workers, such as domestics who seldom even receive social security benefits, and the rest of the labor force (organized labor, white collar, and professional workers).[2]

The magnitude of these benefits was revealed in a study by Macaulay of 1,064 United States firms in 1959. In these firms the average payment for benefits totaled 22.8 per cent of employees' salaries. In a smaller comparative study of 108 identical companies, Macaulay found that payments for benefits increased from 14.7 per cent of salary payments in 1947 to 24.6 per cent in 1959.[3]

Stock option plans alone averaged 21 per cent of executives' cash compensation (salary plus bonus) in 350 companies studied during the 1950's.[4] Although the 1964 Revenue Act slightly reduced the advantage of stock options, the percentage of employees receiving these and other benefits has increased during recent years. For example, the National Industrial Conference Board reports that between 1960 and 1966 the percentage of manufacturers listed on the New York Stock Exchange who had employee stock-purchase plans increased from 12 to 22 per cent; the percentage of gas and utilities companies increased from 26 to 41 per cent, and the percentage of retailers increased from 9 to 23 per cent.[5]

Among the new employee benefits cited by Macaulay

53

are Salk vaccine shots, influenza shots, legal advice and representation, company-financed vacation trips for all employees, a full year's vacation with pay for ten years' service, medical diagnostic service, a car for every employee (including floorsweepers), eye glasses, false teeth, meals for retired employees, and speed reading and college courses.[6]

Nonincome forms of compensation are especially important to top executives whose income is eaten away by high taxes. Table 3–1 shows the percentage of companies surveyed by the National Industrial Conference Board who offer their top executives stock options and deferred compensation plans. Of 1,271 companies surveyed, 12 per cent of the companies' three highest paid executives received estimated annual pensions at age sixty-five of more than $50,000.[7]

Not only highly paid executives benefit from pension plans. Sears Roebuck and Company's thrift-pension fund, whose assets have been invested in the company's common stock, has yielded spectacular employee benefits. Through the pension system, one Sears' clerk, who retired in 1956 after thirty-five years of service and a final salary of $3,500 a year, accumulated $98,000 of Sears common stock. According to the Bureau of Labor Statistics, ". . . her total contributions to the fund were $2,700. Since dividends average about 5 per cent, her retirement income after payment of taxes is greater than her salary while working, and her capital of $98,000 remains untouched!"[8]

A broader survey by the Chamber of Commerce

TABLE 3-1 Employee Benefits of Three Highest Paid Executives in 1,271 Companies, 1967[a]

Type of Compensation	Type of Business					
	Manufacturing (672 companies)	Retail Trade (63 companies)	Gas and Electric Utilities (105 companies)	Commercial Banking (208 banks)	Life Insurance (149 carriers)	Fire, Marine, and Casualty Insurance (74 carriers)
Executive Bonus Awards						
% of companies paying	69	54	8	38	24	34
% of salary	37	50	8	8	10	10
Executive Stock Options						
% of companies with qualified stock option plans	7 75	75	15	23	33	—
Deferred Compensation Plans[b]						
% of companies with deferred compensation contracts for executives	33	60	21	22	17	—
% of companies with deferred profit-sharing plan	24	40	—	57	16	—
Pension benefits— median % of salary	38	34	43	45	43	—
Median annual pension at age 65	$26,000	$25,300	$24,500	$19,000	$16,100	—

[a]Harland Fox, *Top Executive Compensation*, National Industrial Conference Board, Studies in Personnel Policy No. 213 (New York: National Industrial Conference Board, 1969). The manufacturing, retail trade, and gas and electric utilities are represented by practically all of the companies in these types of businesses with securities listed on the New York Stock Exchange. Commercial banking is represented by a sample of all banks with $100 million or more in deposits. Life insurance and fire, marine, and casualty insurance carriers are represented by samples of all companies with 200 or more employees.

[b]A deferred compensation plan is defined as any arrangement that provides for company payments to an executive after he retires.

[c]Fox, *op. cit.*, p. 80.

indicates the general importance of fringe benefits. From 1929 to 1959 payments for employee benefits rose almost seven times as rapidly as payments for employee salaries.[9] New or liberalized fringe benefits were negotiated in settlements that affected 80 per cent of the 2.1 million workers covered by major union contracts that were concluded during the first six months of 1960.[10]

Who gets fringe benefits and how much of them very much affects the distribution of "the command over resources." A given income level does not assure a particular level of fringe benefits. These wage or occupationally connected benefits, as Titmuss has pointed out, have to be included in estimating economic well-being. Unfortunately, there is poor reporting of fringe benefits in relation to income levels.[11]

STABILITY OF INCOME

The confidence that income is assured for all of the year is an important amenity apart from the level of income and nonincome compensation. The assured and stable income of lower white-collar persons is becoming the principal differentiating dimension between them and blue collar workers, who frequently earn higher incomes. For white collar workers, obtaining income in predictable weekly or monthly amounts helps them make decisions governing their activities. Variations in income can be viewed in two ways:

variations within a year and variations between years. To what extent the income of the poor is stable over the year is unclear. The irregular economy of the poor would suggest that even within the low level of income of the poor sizable variations occur in monthly receipts.[12] While some of the poor, such as those persons on welfare, have a somewhat assured but low income, many have an uncertain and unpredictable income that is dependent on economic circumstances and their wits. Data on the within-a-year income stream of various groups of the poor would be useful.

The variations of income over the years are obviously more important than the within-year changes.[13] It is possible to conceptualize income inadequacy in terms of a lifetime rather than a year. In this perspective, the poor would be those families whose lifetime income is below a lifetime poverty-income line.

No matter what income approach is used, are the poor the same group from year to year, except for a relative few who escape? Or does the composition of poverty constantly change, with some falling in and a greater number climbing out? Or do many of those who escape one year move up only to the near-poor level and then fall back into poverty in succeeding years? Is there a pull-out–fall-back syndrome, with families moving back and forth across the poverty line, never much above or below?

Data gathered by the Survey Research Center (see Table 3–2) reveal considerable mobility between the bottom third and the other two-thirds of the spending

TABLE 3-2 Positions of Spending Unit Heads in Income Distributions of Earlier Years, 1928-1960

Group Aged 55 to 64 in Early 1961

1955 position (per cent)

1960 position (per cent)	Bottom third	Middle third	Top third	Total
Bottom third	69	27	6	100
Middle third	30	51	18	100
Top third	0	24	75	100
Total	100	100	100	

1947 position (per cent)

1960 position (per cent)	Bottom third	Middle third	Top third	Total
Bottom third	57	30	15	100
Middle third	33	42	24	100
Top third	9	27	63	100
Total	100	100	100	

1940 position (per cent)

1960 position (per cent)	Bottom third	Middle third	Top third	Total
Bottom third	54	30	18	100
Middle third	33	39	24	100
Top third	12	33	62	100
Total	100	100	100	

1928 position (per cent)

1960 position (per cent)	Bottom third	Middle third	Top third	Total
Bottom third	51	27	21	100
Middle third	30	39	30	100
Top third	18	33	51	100
Total	100	100	100	

Group Aged 45 to 54 in Early 1961

1955 position (per cent)

1960 position (per cent)	Bottom third	Middle third	Top third	Total
Bottom third	69	24	9	100
Middle third	27	51	21	100
Top third	3	27	69	100
Total	100	100	100	

1947 position (per cent)

1960 position (per cent)	Bottom third	Middle third	Top third	Total
Bottom third	60	21	20	100
Middle third	30	48	24	100
Top third	9	30	57	100
Total	100	100	100	

1940 position (per cent)

1960 position (per cent)	Bottom third	Middle third	Top third	Total
Bottom third	51	27	21	100
Middle third	30	42	27	100
Top third	15	33	54	100
Total	100	100	100	

Group Aged 35 to 44 in Early 1961

1955 position (per cent)

1960 position (per cent)	Bottom third	Middle third	Top third	Total
Bottom third	63	27	12	100
Middle third	27	48	24	100
Top third	12	24	63	100
Total	100	100	100	

1947 position (per cent)

1960 position (per cent)	Bottom third	Middle third	Top third	Total
Bottom third	45	30	24	100
Middle third	27	39	33	100
Top third	24	33	45	100
Total	100	100	100	

SOURCE: Calculated from Survey Research Center, University of Michigan, *1961 Survey of Consumers Finances* (Ann Arbor, Mich.: University of Michigan Press, 1962), p. 76, table 5-3.

unit heads. Of spending unit heads aged fifty-five to sixty-four, who were in the bottom third of the income distribution in 1960, only 69 per cent were in the bottom third in 1955, and 51 per cent were in that bracket in 1928. Of those who had incomes in the bottom third in 1928, 51 per cent were in the bottom, 30 per cent were in the middle, and 18 per cent were in the top third in 1960. Obviously, there is much more mobility than is implied in most discussions of the poverty population.

The questions remain, however, "Who moved?" and "How far did they move?" Did families at the bottom of the lowest third experience the same amount of mobility as those at the top of the third? Is there a group in the low-income bracket who do not experience much improvement, while the rest of the poor in any year is made up of families who are only temporarily in poverty? To what extent does a family move across the poverty line because of a demographic shift (for instance, a child marrying at the age of eighteen and leaving the family), which may not reflect great changes in family well-being?[14] Is movement out of poverty caused by additional wage earners, income gains of the main wage earner, or improved transfer payments?

Only a longitudinal study of family income employing a cohort (the same group) that is studied over time with an oversampling of the poor and near-poor can provide answers to many of these important questions. Fortunately, under an Office of Economic Opportunity grant, James Morgan and James Smith have recently begun a five- to six-year longitudinal study of a sample of 5,000 families, composed of 2,000 low-income families taken as a subsample from a 1967 Census survey and a national cross-section of 3,000 families drawn from the University of Michigan's Survey Research Center sampling frame. This "Survey of Economic Opportunity" will provide longitudinal data not only on economic well-being but also on economic behavior and economic attitudes.[15]

The policy implications of income mobility are very important. Should attention be concentrated on those who are potentially mobile to give them a secure hold on the nonpoor rungs of the income ladder? Or should attention be focused on those who have long been at the bottom of the ladder? If the poor are not a stable group, are the present policies concerned with breaking "the culture of poverty" well aimed?

The discussions in the following chapters inadequately mirror the issue of shifting and permanent groups in poverty. The problem of minimum levels in various areas of well-being is enormously complicated by the existence of large numbers who are temporarily below the poverty level.

GOALS

A specific timetable of income inequality reduction is needed. Without clear-cut targets we cannot assess progress.[16] In income, we urge that the nation set as a goal the reduction of the number of families below the budget-standard poverty line to 5 per cent by 1975. (The line should move in relation to prices and general economic advance.) In addition, we should seek to expand the share of income that goes to the bottom 20 per cent of the population by at least 2 to 3 per cent in the next ten years—from 5.4 per cent in 1967 to 8 or 9 per cent in 1977. Specific targets should be set up for other dimensions of well-being as well.

While a major part of the income problem of black citizens is affected by efforts to reduce poverty, not all of it is. The black problem is clearly an issue of inequality between black and white incomes. In the late 1960's, considerable progress was made: the ratio of nonwhite to white income increased from 53 per cent in 1963 to 62 per cent in 1967, an increase of approximately 2¼ per cent a year.[17] This gain should continue so that by 1979, black income would be not less than 89 per cent of white income.

NOTES

1. Cf. Donna Allen, *Fringe Benefits: Wages or Social Obligation?* (Ithaca, N.Y.: Cornell University Press, 1964); Joseph Krislov, "Employee-Benefit Plans, 1954–62," *Social Security Bulletin* (April 1964); U.S. Department of Health, Education and Welfare, Social Security Administration, Division of the Actuary, *Analysis of Benefits Under 26 Selected Private Pension Plans*, Actuarial

Study No. 56 (January 1963); National Industrial Conference Board, "Discount Privileges for Employees," *Studies in Personnel Policy*, No. 207 (New York: National Industrial Conference Board, 1967); "Public Policy and Private Programs, A Report to the President on Private Employee Retirement Plans," *President's Committee on Corporate Pension Funds and Other Private Retirement and Welfare Programs* (Washington, D.C.: U.S. Government Printing Office, January 1965), p. 62.

2. Kleinmann notes seven factors which account for increases in employee benefits during the past three decades:

(1) The government's anti-inflation wage stabilization programs enacted during World War II and the Korean conflict limited wage increases but did not prohibit reasonable employee insurance and retirement benefits. (2) The excess profits taxes on corporations made it possible for employers to put more earnings into employee benefits. (3) The Internal Revenue Act of 1942 exempted from federal income tax the employer's cost of bona fide pension and profit-sharing plans approved by the United States Treasury Department. (4) Two court decisions in 1948 upheld the National Labor Relations Board rulings which established that pension and welfare plans were proper subjects for collective bargaining. [*Inland Steel Company* vs. *NLRB 170 F (2d) 247* (1958); and *W. W. Cross and Company* vs. *NLRB 170 F (2d) 285* (1948).] (5) Enlightened management, on the basis of research in the area of employee morale, has provided many benefits in efforts to establish a "smooth working team" and to improve employer-employee relationships. (6) The expansion of various state and federal welfare measures such as social security, workmen's compensation and unemployment compensation has tended to

foster increasing union and employee preoccupation with these and other types of benefits. Employers are often expected to supplement governmental provisions. (7) Basic humanitarian and social decisions in line with cultural trends of the past decade have influenced the number and variety of benefits made available to employees in addition to salary. [J. H. Kleinmann, *Fringe Benefits of Public School Personnel* (New York: Columbia University Press, 1962), pp. 8–9.]

3. H. H. Macaulay, Jr., *Fringe Benefits and Their Federal Tax Treatment* (New York: Columbia University Press, 1959), pp. 13, 15, 26, 28.
4. William Bowen, "Executive Compensation: The 'New Wave,'" *Fortune* (November 1964), p. 176. Cf. Wilbur G. Lewellen, *Executive Compensation in Large Industrial Corporations* (New York: National Bureau of Economic Research, 1965).
5. National Industrial Conference Board, *Employee Stock Purchase Plans, Studies in Personnel Policy*, No. 206 (New York: National Industrial Conference Board, 1967), pp. 1, 2. In about 12 per cent of the NYSE companies' plans, the company contributed to the purchase of the stock (typically 20 or 25 cents for every dollar an employee put in). The basic advantage of a stock option plan is the special tax treatment provided for stock purchased. Under the 1964 Revenue Act (Section 423b) there is no taxable income to the employee when he purchases the stock, even though the purchase price may then be well below the market price at the time of purchase; and, if the employee does not sell the stock within two years after the date of grant or within six months after the date of purchase, the gain on the sale

of stock is a long-term capital gain, except that there is some ordinary income if the option price was less than 100 per cent of market.

6. Macaulay, *op. cit.*, p. 15.

7. Harland Fox, "Top Executive Compensation," National Industrial Relations Board, *Studies in Personnel Policy*, No. 213 (New York: National Industrial Conference Board, 1969), p. 80.

8. U.S. Department of Labor, Bureau of Labor Statistics, *Economic Forces in the U.S.A. in Facts and Figures, 1957* (Washington, D.C., 1957).

9. These benefits, in the form of employer payments, include (1) legally required payments (social security, unemployment, and workmen's compensation); (2) pension and welfare payments (various group insurances, termination pay allowances, company discounts, savings and stock plans); (3) payments for rest periods and travel time; (4) payments for time not worked (sick leave, vacations, holidays, leave for military or personal reasons); (5) payments for other items (profit-sharing, bonuses). Chamber of Commerce of the United States, *Fringe Benefits, 1959*, revised ed. (Washington, D.C.: The Chamber of Commerce, 1960), p. 33.

10. U.S. Department of Labor, Bureau of Labor Statistics, *Current Wage Developments*, No. 154 (October 1960), p. 4.

11. Richard M. Titmuss, *Income Distribution and Social Change* (London: Allen and Unwin, Ltd., 1962); Titmuss, *Essays on the Welfare State* (New Haven: Yale University Press, 1959).

12. Louis A. Ferman, "Manpower Adaptation—Problematic Social Conditions" (1966, manuscript); S. M. Miller and

Martin Rein, "Barriers to the Employment of the Disadvantaged," *Manpower Report of the President, 1968* (Washington, D.C.: U.S. Government Printing Office, 1968).

13. Otis Dudley Duncan has redirected our attention to this problem.

14. The Office of Economic Opportunity has found that "among 892,000 unmarried dropouts aged 14–19 in *nonpoor* families [according to SSA criteria] in 1965, 92,000 were in families that would have been poor without the dropouts' earnings. These families contained altogether 409,000 persons. A successful program persuading these 92,000 dropouts to return to school would end their annual earnings of $81,000,000 and would drop 409,000 persons below the poverty level." Office of Economic Opportunity, "Dimensions of Poverty in 1964–1965–1966" (draft), December 10, 1968, stencil, p. 16.

15. For a report on some early findings from the first wave of the panel study and for the proposed research design of the study see James N. Morgan and James D. Smith, "Measures of Economic Well-Offness and Their Correlates," *American Economic Review*, LIX, No. 2 (May 1969), 450–460. The measures of economic status will include "family money income, net real income needs, and "well-offness" (net real income needs) times leisure. The measures of economic behavior will include "income increasing acts, connectedness to information and help, evidence of time horizon, risk avoidance, real earning acts, and economizing." Measures of attitudes will include "ambition and aspiration [verbal], sense of personal efficacy, trust in others, and self-reported time

horizon and planning." There will also be measures of past geographical mobility, background problems, and current problems and handicaps.

16. One such set of targets was suggested by the "Freedom Budget." It had seven basic objectives:

(1) To restore full employment as rapidly as possible, and to maintain it thereafter, for all able and willing to work, and for all whom adequate training and education would make able and willing. . . . (2) To assure adequate incomes for those employed. . . . (3) To guarantee a minimum adequacy level of income to all those who cannot or should not be gainfully employed. . . . (4) To wipe out the slum ghettos, and provide a decent home for every American family, within a decade. . . . (5) To provide, for all Americans, modern medical care and educational opportunity up to the limits of their abilities and ambitions, at costs within their means. . . . (6) To overcome other manifestations of neglect in the public sector, by purifying our airs and waters, and bringing our transportation systems and natural resource development into line with the needs of a growing population and an expanding economy. . . . (7) To unite sustained full employment with sustained full production and high economic growth. This is essential, in order that "freedom from want" may be achieved, not by robbing Peter to pay Paul, but under conditions which bring progress to all. [A. Philip Randolph Institute, A "Freedom Budget" for All (October 1966).]

17. U.S. Bureau of the Census, Current Population Report, Series P-60, No. 59, April 18, 1969, Table 3, p. 23.

4
Assets and the Future: Inequalities in the Distribution of Wealth

Current income is an inadequate indicator of the economic position of a family. First, it does not provide an adequate basis for comparing poor and nonpoor groups since some of the income of the nonpoor is received in ways that are purposely designed to appear as nonincome in order to reduce taxation (for example, capital gains). Second, current income inadequately reflects the future command over resources. Savings and pension accumulations are important in the future picture. Further, they affect present satisfactions by providing confidence about the future.[1] Third, past expenditures affect present well-being, as in the case of household furnishings. Fourth, income does not always adequately reflect the character of housing. Fifth, the aged with low incomes (and others who temporarily have low incomes) may have nonpoverty levels of living because of the use of their accumulated assets.

Consequently, in this chapter we discuss a variety of items under the loose appellation of assets. (We do not discuss capital gains since they are included in the discussions of income level.) For symmetry as much as for substance, we have included housing under assets, thereby treating rental units as though they, too, were owner-occupied. Other assets are consumer durables, savings, and insurance.

HOUSING

There are two ways of thinking about housing goals. One is in terms of relativities: How close to "average" levels should the existence of the poor be? For example, should the housing space available to the poor have a minimum level of half of the dwelling space per unit of the nonpoor? A second approach is in terms of presumably scientifically derivable standards of need and subsistence. Clearly, this is what is implied in the budget analyses of food needs. In housing a minimal public health standard of density per room has been constructed. This standard is regarded as scientific rather than cultural or political.[2]

The Bureau of the Census in 1960 used certain visible defects to classify housing as *deteriorating* or *dilapidated*.[3] It also gathered data on water supply, toilet and bathing facilities, source of water, and sewage disposal. By Census criteria, 16 per cent of all housing units were classified as either deteriorating or dilapidated in 1960. Families with incomes under $2,000 are nearly two and a half times as likely to be living in such substandard dwelling places as persons in the total population.[4]

Unfortunately, any assessment of changes over time must be very rough because of the change in the Census definition of substandard housing.[5] Oscar Ornati, comparing trends in the percentage of income groups living in any type of substandard housing, estimates that the lowest income group had the least proportionate improvement in housing between 1950 and 1960.[6] On the other hand, it should be noted that 74 per cent of home owners with incomes under $3,000 lived in sound housing in 1959,[7] and three per cent had houses valued at $25,000 or more in 1967.[8]

When we move beyond standards of sheer adequacy to broader criteria of space, facilities, and housing style, the differences between the poor and nonpoor become more marked. On the financial side, 30 per cent of the houses owned by nonfarm families with incomes under $3,000 were valued at under $5,000, as compared with only 9 per cent of those owned by all nonfarm home-owning families in 1963.[9] Only 46 per cent of the families in the lowest income quintile owned their own homes in 1964,[10] as compared with 86 per cent of families in the highest income quintile.

The poor put a higher percentage of their income into

housing,[11] but do the poor get less for their housing dollars? The data are lacking here. The unavailability of insurance in poor housing areas indicates that low-income families attain little security for their housing dollars. The poor are also less able to maintain or enhance their housing investment.[12] The unavailability of loan funds for low-income persons as well as the low income itself make financing of expensive repairs or additions almost impossible.

The housing of nonwhites, regardless of income level, is considerably less adequate than that of whites. Cutright reports:

Among nonwhite (urban) families, the level in adequate housing using the (Census) rigorous standard is, on the average, 32.4 per cent below the average for (urban) whites —54.3 per cent of all nonwhite families are in housing meeting all criteria compared to 86.7 per cent of whites. Although the proportion of nonwhites adequately housed rises from 40.6 to a high of 74.7 (in the $8,000–9,999 interval), the high income nonwhite family is less likely to be in adequate housing than the white families in the lowest income intervals.[13]

The subsidy system is believed to even out the differences between the poor and nonpoor. However, a full view of subsidies, which includes foregone taxes as well as direct transfers, reveals that the nonpoor benefit more from federal housing activity than the poor! If the loss in taxes resulting from the deductability of interest

70

payments on mortgages is compared with direct housing subsidies to the poor, the former is two and a half times the latter; the nonpoor have federal housing benefits of $2.9 billion, the poor have $820 million.[14] (Indirect benefits to the nonpoor of FHA government insurance, which lowers interest charges, are not included in these calculations.)

The poorest persons benefit very little from federal housing expenditures. They are usually ineligible for public housing because they have very low incomes, present housekeeping problems, or live in areas where public housing is very scarce.[15] In an analysis of four New York City housing projects, Ornati found that on the average the median educational attainment of household heads was higher in housing projects than in adjoining tracts. Nearly half the families who occupied public housing in 1963 were not poor.[16]

In May 1968, New York City liberalized its standards for admission to low-income housing. The old standards, similar to those which still exist in many cities, illustrate the bewildering complexity that may characterize the admissions process. Under the old system, a family whose members fell into any of twenty-one behavior categories was considered a "potential problem," whose application warranted further study by the authority's social service division. The consequent evaluation process took so long that if a family were referred to the social service division, the chances of its getting an apartment were remote. These behavior categories included out-of-wedlock children, alcoholism, use of narcotics, "a record of antisocial behavior," membership in a "violent teenage gang," a history of poor rent payments, frequent separations of husband and wife, a common-law relationship, mental illness that required hospitalization, "unusually frequent" residence changes, poor housekeeping standards "including lack of furniture," "obnoxious conduct" in applying for public housing, and whatever other traits might indicate future trouble.[17]

Numerous recommendations have been made to reduce the housing problems of the poor, but implementation of these recommendations has been very slow. The National Advisory Commission on Civil Disorders in 1968 called for 6 million new housing units in the next five-year period and an increase in the rent-paying capability of low-income households.[18] Congress passed into law the less ambitious goals of another presidential study group, the Kaiser Committee, and then cut back on their authorized funding.[19] During the 1950's 4 million new dwelling units were built in U.S. central cities while 1.5 million units were destroyed.[20] In 1969 the federal government spent for all housing and community development programs about half of the expenditures for highways.[21]

CONSUMER DURABLES

Today consumer durables are an important component of the level of living. Current income inadequately

72

indicates the command over resources of this kind. We believe that enormous variations exist in the possession of durables among low-income families, but information is very spotty. Interpretations of the meaning of possessions have added to the confusion.

One of the problems in ascertaining whether working-class families were becoming "middle class" was the assumption that to own certain objects indicated a zeal for the middle-class value system. Aside from the imputation of a peculiar status concern in purchases, this reasoning suffered from an inadequate realization that better-off families were moving much beyond working-class families in consumer purchases (when workers' families were buying toasters, middle-class families were moving on to bun warmers and the like).[22]

Similarly, one is easily surprised at the variety and cost of the household appliances that are available to the poor. In New York City 95 per cent of low-income families have television sets.[23] By contrast, however, the nonpoor have made significant gains. They use planes to visit distant relatives, while video-tape machines automatically record the television programs missed when away from home. Two or three vacations away from home per year may now be accepted as standard.[24]

Comparisons between the poor and nonpoor should take into consideration the inferior quality of consumer durables that are offered to the poor. For example, many of the washing machines of low-income families are old hand washers that are in need of major repairs, as is obvious on the the porches of homes in the hollows of Appalachia. Also, the poor pay more, so that expenditure is an inadequate indicator of value.

What standard of consumer durables should be used for the poverty line? One is in terms of minimal needs, which home economists and other specialists can define: What is the supply of durables that every family should have? In essence, many durables are no longer in the luxury class. For example, a refrigerator might be considered as a basic durable minimum. In some areas of the country, a car might be. Home furnishings (beds, chairs, tables, and some pictures) might be another.

Constructing a minimum durables standard would require that attention be given to the average durable goods possessions of nonpoor families, and that some estimate be made of what is a reasonable gap in terms of service and aesthetics. Presumably, the policy that flows from this approach will ensure that each family has the ingredients of the minimum durables standards. Welfare departments have constructed such budgets, though at very low levels, and without permitting families choices among the kinds of items they would like to have. A different approach would maximize the choices among the low income. The dollar value of the durables of the nonpoor would be the basis of a standard of durables for the poor. The latter would have funds available to them up to perhaps one-half of the value of the nonpoor's durables and could spend the available amounts on whatever durables they pleased.

74

SAVINGS

Liquid assets are not only an important protector against emergencies; they can also break the fall into poverty. For want of savings, any emergency drains a low-income family, and debt ensues; the family may have to move and change employment. Savings not only provide some psychological security; they are also an important instrument in maintaining or improving economic conditions.

Savings are obviously concentrated: In 1967, 62 per cent of families with incomes of less than $3,000 had no savings at all, while 60 per cent of families with incomes above $15,000 had more than $6,000 in their savings accounts.[25] The form of asset holding is important because it affects the possibility of assets increasing in value or yielding income. In 1967, 51 per cent of families with incomes of $15,000 or more had stock holdings valued at $1,000 or more; 4 per cent of families with incomes under $3,000 held stocks above this level. (Most of these families were headed by persons over sixty-five years of age.)[26]

From the point of view of inequality, savings and other forms of assets are important. When income alone is considered, then the differences between the poor and nonpoor appear narrower than they are. For example, the asset level of the aged nonpoor not only puts them in a higher income bracket than the aged poor, but provides a stream of income over the future. (Many assets are forms of deferred income.)

What should be the goal in the area of liquid assets? For low-income persons a minimum level of liquid assets should be twice the weekly income. Achievement of this goal is difficult since the poor might well utilize savings for current needs; thus a long-run asset-building program would become a current-income program.

INSURANCE

The average American who lives to the age of sixty-five can expect to live for another fifteen years. A tenth or more of the current income of many individuals is devoted to providing security for their later years. Thus, the command over future resources is a major concern of Americans today. It affects not only the calculation of current income but the satisfactions and security derived from earnings.

The present methods of protecting against old age deepen inequalities: *the concentration of income among the aged is greater than it is among younger age groups or in the nation as a whole.* In 1964, the upper 20 per cent of families headed by a person over sixty-four years old received 52 per cent of that group's aggregate income as compared with 41 per cent received by the upper fifth of the nation as a whole and 37 per cent of the age group twenty-four to thirty-four.[27] In 1964, less than 0.5 per cent of families with incomes under $3,000, as compared with 2 per cent of all families, had savings in the form of retirement funds

76

or old-age pensions.[28] Similarly, in 1967 life-insurance ownership varied from 50 per cent among families with incomes of less than $3,000 to 98 per cent among those with incomes between $10,000 and $15,000.[29]

Although in recent years Congress has tended to adjust upward OASDI benefits proportionately with increases in the consumer price index, a special cost-of-living index for the aged should be constructed as advocated by Margaret Gordon. This index might make a marked difference because of pronounced increases in the cost of certain items, such as medical care, that figure prominently in the budgets of elderly people.[30]

The system of transfer through public assistance only partially reduces the inequalities of private savings and returns and the distribution of social security and private pension benefits.[31] With the extension of life and the concern about the future, deferred income in the form of pensions should be an important consideration in today's assessment of economic well-being.

A difficult question emerges if pension accumulations are included as an important aspect of one's standard of living before age sixty-five. The public welfare system provides aid to the aged with low incomes; in 1965, 4.1 million aged (persons over sixty-four) received Old Age Survivors, Disability and Health Insurance; 2.1 million received Public Assistance in the form of Old Age Assistance.[32] Can we consider different levels of pension accumulations today as important when welfare will be available for those who are poor in their old age? One response to this is that welfare is stigmatizing.

Another is that welfare payments are so low that while an income "floor" is available, it does not provide much security and confidence about the future. Depending on public authorities to provide a small amount of money to keep one going is quite different from having a guaranteed future. In reality, even this low welfare floor is only a grating: 22 per cent of the aged still fall beneath the poverty line.[33]

NOTES

1. The importance of supplementary benefits is reflected in collective bargaining for union contracts. In 1966, 32 per cent of union establishments and 40 per cent of nonunion establishments liberalized or established one or more new supplementary practices, such as health and welfare plans, pensions, paid funeral leave, vacations and holidays. William Davis and L. M. David, "Pattern of Wage and Benefit Changes in Manufacturing," *Monthly Labor Review* (February 1968), p. 46.

2. In general, we support the use of relativities rather than absolute standards. Fixed standards have the political value of being beyond politics and feasibility, but we doubt that over a term of years standards can move up rapidly to keep pace with an economy that is swiftly expanding. In general, our aim is to have forthright discussions of inequalities rather than improvements through subterfuge. We do not have confidence in subterfuge as an enduring political device.

3. See U.S. Census of Housing, *Metropolitan Housing*, Final Report, HC (2)-1, A (1960), 62.

Deteriorating housing needs more repair than would be provided in the course of regular maintenance. Such housing has one or more defects of an intermediate nature that must be corrected if the unit is to continue to provide safe and adequate shelter.

Dilapidated housing does not provide safe and adequate shelter and in its present condition endangers the health, safety, or well-being of the occupants. Such housing has one or more critical defects; or has a combination of intermediate defects in sufficient number or extent to require considerable repair or rebuilding; or is of inadequate original construction. The defects are either so critical or so widespread that the structure should be extensively repaired, rebuilt, or torn down.

It is doubtful whether these concepts are adequate for the post-World War II period.

4. Thirty-nine per cent of those with incomes under $2,000 as compared with 20 per cent of the $3,000 to $3,999 income category lived in substandard units.

5. Deteriorated housing with plumbing was classified as substandard in 1960 but not in 1950. Census takers and other observers have also been found to have difficulty judging housing quality.

6. Oscar Ornati, *Poverty Amid Affluence* (New York: The Twentieth Century Fund. 1966), p. 179.

7. Sixty-one per cent of families and individuals with incomes under $3,000 living in rented units had "sound" housing in 1959. The $3,000 line is, of course, a rough measure of poverty for it includes retired persons who once had considerably higher incomes; the rich man who has suffered a temporary loss as well as the poor. U.S. Census of Housing, *op. cit.*, pp. 1–6, Table A–4.

8. Survey Research Center, University of Michigan, *1967 Survey of Consumer Finances* (Ann Arbor, Mich.: University of Michigan Press, 1968), p. 52.

9. Survey Research Center, University of Michigan, *1963 Survey of Consumer Finances* (Ann Arbor, Mich.: University of Michigan Press, 1964), p. 88.

10. Survey Research Center, University of Michigan, *1965 Survey of Consumer Finances* (Ann Arbor, Mich.: University of Michigan Press, 1966), p. 117.

11. Survey Research Center, University of Michigan, *1964 Survey of Consumer Finances* (Ann Arbor, Mich.: University of Michigan Press, 1965), p. 31. In 1964, nonfarm rent-paying families with incomes less than $3,000 paid a median monthly rent of $45, as compared with $65 paid by those with incomes of $3,000 to $4,999. Cf. Alvin L. Schorr, *Slums and Social Insecurity* (Washington, D.C.: Department of Health, Education and Welfare, SSA, Division of Research and Statistics, Research Report No. 1, 1963).

12. *Ibid.*, p. 35. Only 18 per cent of nonfarm families with incomes under $3,000, as compared with 34 per cent of the total nonfarm population, had housing addition and repair expenditures of over $49 in 1964.

13. Phillips Cutright, "Income and Family Events" (Paper presented at American Academy of Arts and Sciences Conference on Income and Poverty, Boston, May 16, 1969), p. 33.

14. Alvin L. Schorr, "National Community and Housing Policy," *Social Service Review* (1965), p. 434; Alvin L. Schorr, *Explorations in Social Policy* (New York: Basic Books, 1968).

15. Alvin L. Schorr, "Housing" (August 1965, manuscript),

p. 6. Almost 60 per cent of substandard housing is in rural areas.

16. David Caplovitz, *The Poor Pay More* (New York: The Free Press, 1963).

17. The following six potential-problem criteria are included under the new procedure: a history of recent serious criminal activity, a pattern of violent behavior, confirmed drug addiction, conviction for rape or sexual deviation, grossly unsanitary or hazardous housekeeping, and a record of serious disturbance of neighbors, destruction of property or other disruptive or dangerous behavior. *The New York Times*, May 12, 1968, p. 5.

18. The National Advisory Commission on Civil Disorders.

19. The President's Committee on Urban Housing, *A Decent Home* (Washington, D.C.: U.S. Government Printing Office, 1969).

20. Urban America and the Urban Coalition, *One Year Later* (New York: Frederick A. Praeger, 1969), pp. 46–47.

21. *Ibid.*, pp. 51–52.

22. S. M. Miller and Frank Riessman, "Are Workers Middle Class?" *Dissent* (1962).

23. The visible ownership of television sets among the poor ought not blind us to the differentiation which exists in the ownership patterns of the poor and nonpoor. In 1966, 9 per cent of families with incomes under $3,000 and 2 per cent of those with incomes over $15,000 owned no major appliances (television, refrigerator, washing machine, cooking range, or air-conditioner); conversely, 9 per cent of those with less than $3,000 and 47 per cent of those with incomes over $15,000 owned five or more major appliances. The appliances of low-

income families were also older and had had more repairs than those of the higher-income families. Survey Research Center, *1967 Survey of Consumer Finances*, pp. 114–115.

24. Seventy-three per cent of families with incomes over $15,000 as compared with 18 per cent of those with less than $3,000, took vacations in 1966. Survey Research Center, *1967 Survey of Consumer Finances*, p. 117.

25. Survey Research Center, *1967 Survey of Consumer Finances*, p. 79.

26. *Ibid.*, p. 129.

27. U.S. Bureau of the Census, *Trends in the Income of Families and Persons in the United States: 1947–1964*, Technical Paper No. 17 by Mary F. Henson (Washington, D.C.: U.S. Government Printing Office, 1967), p. 182.

28. Survey Research Center, *1967 Survey of Consumer Finances*, p. 128. At each income level persons who contribute to private pension funds save more in a given year than those who do not contribute and tend to devote the same fraction of their income to life insurance. Margaret S. Gordon, *The Economics of Welfare Policies* (New York: Columbia University Press, 1963), p. 50.

29. Survey Research Center, *1967 Survey of Consumer Finances*, p. 124.

30. Gordon, *op. cit.*, p. 55.

31. No one who lives out the fifteen years of past sixty-five expectancy has paid into social security as much as he receives from it. The payment from social security is based more on the symbolism of contribution than on actual contribution. Musgrave found that in 1954 effective social insurance tax rates were regressive over the

income distribution as a whole and fairly uniform for tax brackets under $5,000 (Gordon, *op. cit.*, p. 25). Cf. James Morgan, M. H. David, W. J. Cohen, H. E. Brazer, *Income and Welfare in the United States* (New York: McGraw-Hill, 1962); W. Irwin Gillespie, "Effect of Public Expenditures on the Distribution of Income," in Richard Musgrave, ed., *Essays in Fiscal Federalism* (Washington, D.C.: Brookings Institution, 1965); George Bishop, *Tax Burdens and Benefits of Government Expenditures by Income Class, 1961 and 1965* (New York: Tax Foundation, 1967).

32. *Social Security Bulletin* (February 1967), pp. 1, 44.
33. Mollie Orshansky, "More about the Poor in 1964," *Social Security Bulletin* (May 1966), p. 5.

5
Basic Services: The Hidden Multipliers of Income

Income and assets are important components of the command over resources, but they do not include the increasingly important area of services. These services include education and training, health, neighborhood amenities, protection, social services, and transportation. In the high-income society, services comprise a great and increasing proportion of expenditures and furnish important segments of total satisfaction and well-being.

The connection between family income and basic services is close but incomplete. A fairly well-to-do rural family may have inadequate immediate health care because no health center is nearby, while an urban low-income family may have access to an excellent medical teaching center. Or, two families with the same low level of income may live in very different environments—one in an overcrowded area, with few recreational facilities, poor sanitation and garbage control, inadequate police protection, little transportation, the other in a high-density area with outstanding services. For example, in Sweden the poor are better off than in the United States because their low incomes are not associated with poor basic services.

CONCEPTS

Below, we discuss five issues in conceptualizing and measuring basic services: the public-private mix of services; services as amenities or investments; minimum or adequate levels of living as the objectives; output criteria; availability and utilization.

First, basic services are usually associated with the public sector, but this is not inevitable. The growth of fringe benefits in private employment means that the non-public sector provides many basic services. In the United States, many hospital insurance plans and health services are provided by private employers. While the history of the growth of basic services for the poor has to a large extent meant the enlargement of the public sector, this may not be intrinsic to the development of the services. Indeed, conservative groups, such as the Institute of Economic Affairs in England strongly insist that increased reliance on the market will produce more and better basic services.[1] The sharp distinction between public and private sectors may become increasingly useless.

Second, are basic services to be considered as amenities or investments? As amenities, services directly increase the consumption of individuals. They are not means to the attainment of other resources; they are themselves an important component of the level of living. As investments, however, they are ways of improving the capacity of individuals to gain access to resources through the private market; for example, better health services or improved transportation to jobs increase the earning capacity of the individual or family.

The trend of liberal thought is to transmute goals into means. What is desirable as a goal is not defended on that basis but on the contention that it is instrumental to the achievement of other goals. Rationality —the effectiveness of one program to achieve another— supplants desirability—a program that is desired in itself. We strongly doubt that many of the activities characterized as investments in human resources, for example, health programs, are really effective methods to increase earning capacity.[2] Consequently, we regard basic services as amenities rather than as investments in human resources development.

A third problem, discussed earlier, is the question of goals in the area of basic services. Is the objective a minimum or adequate level? Or is the issue that of the relative distribution between those at the bottom and other groups in society? In the second case, it is a question of distribution of resources; in the first, it is a question of standards. Adequacy is the major criterion in a presumably essential program like health services; but as general conditions improve in a society, questions of relative distribution assume greater importance.

Fourth, a particularly sensitive problem is the connection between services and well-being. Do services actually contribute to improved circumstances of life, or is their usefulness overstated? For example, some evidence suggests that personal health services (as contrasted with public health measures such as sewage) do not have a high impact upon physical well-being. Similar questions have been raised about the effectiveness of casework services and psychotherapy.

Since we measure most services by their costs and quantities, we do not have an estimate of their yield, especially to people of different income levels; for the services may yield more to one group than to another. This differential yield could be a product of differences in quality. That which purports to be the same basic service, for example, school education, may vary widely in quality.

Fifth is the issue of the availability of services versus their utilization. To some analysts, the issue is simply that services be available to a particular population. If the group does not use the service for whatever reason, that is its own prerogative; the service organization cannot be condemned for the resultant inequitable distribution of its resources. A contrasting notion is that the issue is actual delivery of the services. Availability of service is not sufficient; direct efforts are needed to

87

cope with the obstacles which result in their low utilization by the poor.

PROCESSES

As the social services grow in the United States, it will be increasingly important for social scientists to concentrate on the processes which influence the effects of organizational activities on clients. Organizational policies and practices, which frequently do not consciously consider individual applicants, largely affect who receives and who does not receive services. Persons who make and administer organizational policy select and process applicants on the basis of how they fit their own and their organization's needs and outlook. Selection and exclusion of potential recipients occur at several points in the contact between agency and the poor client. When analyzing the effectiveness of a social service, we need to evaluate the presentation of the service, the admission process, the completion process, and the aftermath, or what happens to persons following their completion of the service.[3]

Three major questions are involved in the presentation of programs for the poor. First, who is notified of the program? Second, what impression does the program give to its audience? Third, is the program or service accessible to persons who find it appealing and would like to participate in it?

Those individuals who surmount their first hurdle

face admission. What happens to people who apply for a service or a program? How do agencies treat them? Discouraging waiting, intra- and/or inter-agency referral, conditional admittance, and admittance may all be involved in the first selection of an individual for services. In admitting individuals into a program, agencies use a variety of standards. These criteria lead to the exclusion of the poorest persons from the potential benefits of the program. Agencies want to know if the applicant is a good risk and if he is easy to manage. Formal qualifications, such as education, age, permanent residency, and a clear criminal record, also bar many from these programs.[4] In some programs, the periods of testing to determine the appropriateness of the individual for the available service and the periods of waiting for test results may be trying experiences, causing applicants to drop out before they are either admitted or rejected.

Who completes a program, and what is involved in its completion? Those who begin a program differ markedly from those who finish. Selective dropping or pushing out occurs. Completion of a program is conditioned by the effort which an individual must expend to remain in a program, the willingness of the agency to keep the individual, the continuation of the program itself, and the amount of benefit the individual is receiving, believes he is receiving, or will receive from the program. Agencies may make it easier for individuals to remain in their programs by providing transportation and child-care services; also, as in the case of manpower-training programs, they may pay the trainee a small stipend to compensate for the income he may forego during the training and to allow him to maintain himself. Agencies vary in their understanding of and openness to various modes of individual behavior. In some agencies, individuals whose behavior does not conform closely to middle-class styles are encouraged to leave or are dismissed prior to completion. All too frequently, completion of a program is entirely outside of the clients' control because the entire program is terminated by the lack of renewed funding.

The amount of benefit which a client believes he is receiving or will receive from a program depends upon both its mode of presentation and the actual benefits which it confers on him and on others who have progressed further through the program. For example, individuals are more likely to continue with health or training programs if the reason for particular treatment or training is made understandable to them.

The completion stage of some programs offers benefits that the client seeks immediately, while other programs prepare the client to seek post-program benefits. For example, the "new careers" programs allow subprofessionals to work in stimulating jobs as they learn, while other programs require the individual to complete months of training without the guarantee of a job at the end. Individuals are likely to drop out of the latter programs if they see that friends and neighbors who finish before them are unable to obtain jobs or other promised benefits—the final stage in the delivery of services.

90

In evaluating social services, it is not enough merely to ask about the availability of services and the numbers who complete various programs. We must also ask about the aftermath of services. Does anyone benefit from the services? If so, who? How lasting is their benefit? Does the improvement in the individual's life help him obtain other benefits for himself or others?

In the discussion that follows, we deal with four areas of basic services: health, neighborhood amenities, transportation, and legal and social services.

HEALTH

The utilization of health services and definitions of *health* vary among social classes. As Lee explains,

When income is more than adequate for basic needs, one's list of desirables, or even of necessities, can include many values several steps removed from mere survival. One can insist on treatment for physical discomfort, can take measures to provide for future health and prolongation of life, and can afford to think of annual medical examinations as routine. On the other hand, when income is uncertain and not always enough to provide food and shelter, health is likely to be defined as the ability to keep working. Treatment is postponed until acute symptoms or disability preclude work.[5]

The poor of all ages consult doctors, dentists, and medical specialists less frequently than do the nonpoor.[6] The rate of visits to physicians' offices as compared with the use of the telephone or hospital clinic visits also declines with income. Short-stay hospital utilization, in terms of rates of discharge, age for age, is somewhat less for low-income persons than high-income persons.[7] Utilization of immunization and pediatric services has also been found to be inversely related to income.[8] Similarly, the utilization of dental services has been consistently and inversely related to social class.[9]

Do the poor use health services less frequently because they are healthier? The answer is probably no. Charlotte Muller succinctly summarizes the findings: "Identifying the low-income group is tantamount to identifying a high probability of medical need as shown by various indexes of prevalence and severity of disabling illness."[10]

Muller found that although low-income persons (family incomes under $2,000) made less than a third as many dental visits per year as high-income persons (family incomes over $7,000), nearly four times as many low-income persons required extractions when they made dental visits.[11]

Nikias reports that most of the available evidence seems to suggest that the children of low socioeconomic families tend to experience more tooth decay (carious lesions) than children in high socioeconomic families.[12] For instance, in a recent study of dental-caries experience among 3,911 five year old children in Contra Costa County, California, it was found that the children of the higher socioeconomic groups experienced fewer carious lesions than the children in the lower socio-economic groups. This distinction held true whether the basis of socioeconomic status index was the Hollings-head Two-Factor Index of Social Position, family income, father's education, or socioeconomic residential district. Furthermore, the same study showed that the higher the socioeconomic level, the greater the percentage of caries-free children. Thirty-four per cent of the children whose fathers were college graduates as compared with 19 per cent of those whose fathers had completed one to nine years of schooling had no tooth decay.[13]

In the National Health Survey, it was found that although persons with low family incomes have lower rates of hospitalization, they require more days of care when they are hospitalized.[14] Restricted activity days, as well as bed-disability days, are over twice as frequent in the lowest income group as in the highest.[15] The lowest income class also has the highest rates of heart diseases, diabetes mellitus, arthritis, and diseases of female genital organs.[16]

The pattern of mortality rates among the poor is similar to that of illnesses. In major United States cities, higher infant mortality rates generally prevail in non-white areas. Nationally, the gap between death rates for white and nonwhite infants is increasing.[17] Fetal loss varies with instability of income, measured by husband's unemployment history.[18]

The relationship between infrequent health care, poor health, and low income is more intricate than an analysis based solely upon these data would indicate.[19] Income is only one aspect of poverty. The complexity of the interrelationships between the dimensions of poverty and health is demonstrated in Hauser and Kitagawa's analysis of mortality in the United States. Both education and income vary inversely with mortality; however, the opposite is true for men, although educational differentials in mortality are larger than income differentials for women.[20] Education has also been found to be more highly correlated than income with dental visits that involve treatment of severe periodontal disease.[21]

Nikias found that despite the fact that they belonged to a prepayment dental insurance plan, semi-skilled and unskilled workers used dental services only about half as frequently as skilled and clerical workers, and sales, executive, and professional workers used these services.[22] Extractions were the only type of dental service which varied inversely with occupational level.[23] However, there was no substantial difference in the number of dental visits obtained by persons in the three occupational categories *after* they made their first visit.[24]

Nikias interprets these marked differences in the utilization of dental services by persons faced with small or no direct dental cost as reflecting the previous life training of working-class families as compared with middle-class families. She observes that persons without experience of dental care, perhaps because of their families' previous inability to pay for dental services, cannot, without reeducation, be expected to take on new health habits, despite the availability of free care.[25]

Persons who lack health education are frequently unable to identify and care for minor symptoms in time to prevent major medical problems. Lack of experience with professionals also causes these people to hesitate in seeking their help before an ailment is severe. Those who experience difficulty in communicating their needs or feel stigmatized and out of place within professional surroundings delay their return as long as possible.

In some areas of the United States, great strides appear to have been made in health services for the poor, but most regions need enormous improvement.[26] The inequality in the distribution of health services among various regions is particularly striking. New York State, for instance, has 211 doctors per 100,000 population; Mississippi has 74. Massachusetts has 502 professional nurses per 100,000 population; Arkansas has 120.[27] As of 1963, New York had one dentist per 1,220 population; South Carolina had one per 4,292 persons.[28] In areas with shortages of doctors, dentists, and nurses, the poor are generally the first to go without needed treatment. In Mississippi, 99.3 per cent of white births took place in a hospital and were attended by a physician. Of Mississippi Negro births, however, only 53 per cent were in a hospital and attended by a physician; 2 per cent were attended by a physician in the home, and 45 per cent were "other." Infant mortality rates followed the same pattern: the rate for Mississippi whites was 23.6 per 1,000 live births as compared with 49.9 per

1,000 live Negro births.[29] For persons over sixty, Medicare may partially counter the inverse relationship between income and health care; however, for many persons with a history of inadequate health care, Medicare will be too late to be of much assistance.

What criteria are to be used to judge the quality of services? Patient satisfaction? Recovery rates? Professional evaluations? Each has its pitfalls. The difficulties involved in developing these indicators are amplified by questions of professional authority. Nonetheless, a few assessments of professional care have been made. A study of expectant mothers in metropolitan Boston showed that the percentage judged to have received satisfactory medical care rose steadily with income.[30]

Poor treatment is not confined to the poor, nor is excellent care given only to the well-to-do. Sliding scales for fees mean that higher dollar figures for medical expenditures do not necessarily reflect better care. Good health care is frequently distributed on the basis of neither medical nor financial need, but on the basis of the medical interest of the patient's case or the patient's ability to manipulate the system.

Obviously, income affects the ability of a family to obtain medical services for which it must pay and to purchase hospital and surgical insurance that will cover a portion of potential medical expenses. Muller reports, however, that for every dollar spent by consumers, or financed by their premiums and the payments of employers or by insurance carriers on their behalf or by philanthropies, another 25 cents is spent out of the public treasury.[31] Much of this public spending is channeled to the poor, but, as Alvin Schorr has pointed out, the neediest do not necessarily receive their share of the benefits of public programs.[32] Today, data are available only on the utilization of Medicare; it will necessarily be years before the new benefits' effects on illness and mortality rates are known.

What are the goals in health? The goals can be specified in terms of mortality and morbidity. Are health and longevity areas in which our society no longer finds class differences acceptable? We have the odd feeling that American opinion implicitly argues for equality of outcome in health and longevity and for inequality in the distribution of services!

To reduce the disparities among the rich and poor may require more than simply rectifying the distribution of services. In mental retardation, where there are pronounced differences in incidence, the mother's conditions of life during the prenatal period are undoubtedly more important than medical services. Environmental conditions as well as nutritional patterns have long been recognized as affecting health. Health is not only a reflection of health services.

The adequacy of health services is a general problem in our society. Despite enormous expenditures, the United States has fallen behind many other nations in crucial indicators of health. The plight of the poor is directing attention to the general medical situation, with the possibility of improved health services for all.

Neighborhood Amenities

Neighborhood amenities refer to such important influences on the character of a habitat as sanitation control, police and fire protection, recreational facilities, libraries, parks and playgrounds, and the condition of streets and roads. Neighborhood amenities are the conditions that are usually collectively provided for a neighborhood through public expenditures of one kind or another.

A common observation in many large cities is the differences in the sanitation pickup in low-income and in high-income neighborhoods. In low-income neighborhoods, especially those which are not politically important or are opposed to the party in power, sanitation pickup is sporadic, infrequent, and very inadequate. Strongly organized, high-status areas that complain the most are most likely to get satisfactory garbage control. As a result, the poorest persons suffer from inadequate sanitation and garbage control.

A common complaint in many low-income areas is that of inadequate police protection. This complaint is coupled with grievances about police brutality. Arguments about excessive police force do not mean that police aid is not desired.[33] The Ribicoff Senate Hearings on urban problems reported that the citizens of Harlem and Watts are concerned about the inadequate availability of police as well as about the excessive use of force by police. Similarly, a 1968 study of more than 5,000 blacks and whites in 15 major American cities

98

found that 47 per cent of blacks as compared with 31 per cent of whites were "somewhat" or "very dissatisfied" with the quality of police protection in their neighborhoods.[34]

Data across the country on the degree of police availability and activity in low-income areas are hard to obtain. Due to the high incidence of crime in these areas, the general impression is that there is inadequate police protection in these areas. Of course, the underlying issue is to what extent would having more police drastically reduce this crime rate? The kinds and quality of police service are the important issues.[35] The objectives of police service are still being debated, and important new programs have been recommended.

Similarly, the data on the availability of fire protection in low-income areas are very spotty. We know that insurance companies are reluctant to insure in these areas. It would be useful to try to develop some index of police and fire protection which would mirror changes over time in the degree of availability of such facilities.

An adequate measure of recreational facilities is difficult to construct. This is partly because transportation to distant recreational facilities is differentially distributed. Patricia Sexton found that "there are more parks and recreation areas in the upper-income areas of Detroit than in the lower-income areas." The smallest amount of park space per 10,000 people "is found in the oldest part of the city . . . where the lowest-income groups live. In one large section of this area (130,000 population) there are only 2.6 acres of recreation area per 10,000 people—as compared with 30 acres in the highest-income area."[36]

Children in low-income areas tend to be much less mobile than children in upper-income areas. Poorer children (because their parents usually do not have cars or the money for travel, summer camps, or even local bus transportation) are virtually imprisoned in the crowded areas where they live. When recreation facilities in these areas are not adequate, it is very difficult for lower-income children to go elsewhere to find them. Limited evidence on the use of national parks seems to suggest that they are more likely to be used by middle-income people rather than lowest-income people. On the other hand, some ethnic groups, such as the Puerto Ricans, who have a history of outdoor life are probably more likely than other groups to use park facilities. In general, dissatisfaction is high. Campbell and Schuman found that in 1968 both whites and blacks were more dissatisfied with their neighborhoods' parks and playgrounds for children and sports and recreation centers for teenagers than they were with the quality of their public schools.[37]

Museums and libraries seem to be disproportionately used by the nonpoor, although time series data are exceedingly sparse. These expensive facilities tend to be mainly used by a limited segment of a population. It could be argued that this results from attitudes about museums and libraries rather than from questions of effective delivery. Some believe, however, that efforts to decentralize such facilities, and to make them inter-

100

esting and attractive to the poor, might be effective. Thomas Hoving of the Metropolitan Museum of Art argues against museum decentralization, however, on the basis that museums lose the relief they offer from the routine world when they are set up in storefronts. Therefore, his efforts are oriented toward bringing the poor into the central museum. (The Metropolitan Museum of Art's "Harlem on My Mind" photography exhibit in 1969 did attract both youth and adults from Harlem.)

It would be useful to develop cultural indices that would reveal the use of such facilities as museums and libraries. These indices could indicate the degree of success of the concerted policies to deepen the use of these facilities by low-income and poorly educated groups. The use of museums and libraries by socialist-oriented workers in Poland and other European nations suggests that some gains could be made.[38]

Mass Transportation

Mass transportation is more important to the poor than to the nonpoor. Unfortunately, mass transportation has been a major casualty of the post-World War II era. This loss affects the economic and social well-being of the poorly off. Today job opportunities are multiplying in the suburbs, but they are out of reach of the poor in the center city. Low-income persons cannot afford costly long-distance commuting by car and generally lack other transportation alternatives.[39] On the other hand, they cannot afford, or are not permitted because of racial discrimination, to live near the new factories, hospitals, commercial buildings, schools, and stores on the periphery of the city.

A minimum level of access to and information about transportation is particularly important to low-income persons who are searching for jobs. And yet public transportation routes leading from poverty areas to work sites are generally considerably more inconvenient than those leading from the well-to-do neighborhoods of persons who are more likely to possess the alternative of personal transportation. For example, Whittaker points out that most transportation anomalies (a central Brooklyn resident's trip to industrial districts only four miles away is longer and more complicated than a trip to the Bronx some fifteen miles away) relate to journeys between poverty areas and the centers of employment where the poor might find jobs.[40]

Project Labor Market of New York University has made three relatively inexpensive (in comparison with various technological suggestions of other planners) recommendations to improve public transportation service for low-income areas in New York City, which might apply in other cities as well:

1. Create new express bus routes from poverty areas to large industrial complexes (bus, unlike subway, routes are relatively easy to experiment with).
2. Distribute free transfers to remove inequalities in the

fare-structure. (At present, the residents of low-income areas such as Manhattan's Lower East Side have to make numerous transfers on their journey to work.)

3. Increase the quality and dissemination of transit information.[41]

Inadequate transportation is one of the hallmarks today of inequality. With the great geographic mobility of Americans, relatives are far-flung. Social, recreational, and cultural facilities are not available, even if free or low-cost, if transportation is difficult. Mid-twentieth century life depends on adequate transportation.

LEGAL SERVICES

American society prides itself that all persons are equal before the law. In practice, the well-to-do and higher-educated are better treated by judicial officials and have easier access to useful legal services than do the poor. In the case of the law, the goal obviously is that low-income persons should be as well treated as high-income persons, and blacks should be accorded the same treatment as whites. But this would mean an equal distribution of legal services, which is a far cry from our present situation.

Jerome Carlin, after studying lawyers' ethics in New

York City, described the present state of legal services for the poor:

The best trained, most technically skilled, and ethically most responsible lawyers are reserved to the upper reaches of business and society. This leaves the least competent, least well-trained, and least ethical lawyers to the smaller business concerns and lower-income individuals. As a result, the most helpless clients who most need protection are least likely to get it.

The uneven character of legal services, moreover, leads to a highly selective development of the law itself. Those areas that reflect the interest of large corporations and wealthy individuals are most likely to be elaborated; law dealing with the poor and other disadvantaged groups, particularly in the consumer, landlord-tenant, welfare, and domestic relations areas, remains largely neglected and under-developed.

Whatever efforts have been made by leaders of the profession to cope with these problems have been largely ineffective. Lack of leadership is particularly evident in the failure of the organized bar to seek and to support new forms of legal representation that might help in extending legal services to a larger segment of the population.[42]

A series of decisions, such as those in *Gideon* v. *Wainwright,* the *Brotherhood of Railroad Trainmen* v. *Virginia,* and *Miranda* v. *Arizona,* and the surprising success of the Office of Economic Opportunity in promoting legal services for the poor have reduced the disparities between the legal condition and services available to the poor and those available to the nonpoor.[43] However, a gap continues to exist. It is uncertain how wide the gap between the legal condition of the poor and nonpoor is, but as Senator Robert Kennedy said, the poor person continues to look "upon the law as an enemy. . . . For him, it is always taking something away." It would be useful and not impossible to construct and maintain indices of legal treatment and services.[44]

Legal services are only one aspect of the issue of legal rights. Another more difficult and subtle aspect is the equity of the law itself. Better legal services cannot protect the poor from statutes of the sort that prompted Anatole France to sarcastically remark, "The law, in all its majesty, forbids rich as well as poor to sleep under bridges on rainy nights, to beg on the streets and to steal bread."[45] Edgar and Jean Cahn, who are both deeply involved in the development of legal services, argue:

New legal service programs for the poor cannot . . . rest with providing the poor with greater opportunity to use a legal system which the middle class has found to be obsolete, cumbersome—and too expensive in monetary, psychological and temporal terms. Nor can such programs function simply to endow the poor with the ultimate recourse of the middle class—litigation—because the middle class has found recourse to courts to be unsatisfactory either as a final or an intermediary remedy.

Both for the poor and the nonpoor, justice is in short supply. The result is inflation and inflation for the poor does not mean doing without justice. It means injustice.

105

The middle class has found a way of dealing with this inflation. They do not buy legal services—except as a last resort. Instead, they have used the legal profession to develop a set of substitutes—a legal system which operates without benefit of LL.B. wherever possible. . . . In essence, the lawyer acts as the architect of institutions (such as corporations) and as the draftsman of instruments that can be utilized effectively by laymen without continual surveillance and intervention by lawyers. Thus, in the tort field, insurance companies and claims adjusters do much of the work of lawyers. . . . In the criminal law, low visibility decisions of an essentially consensual sort have largely replaced formal prosecution. . . . Thus, for instance, the policeman does not make a formal arrest of a middle-class youth. The *quid pro quo* is that the father agrees that this behavior is a matter for parental concern and attention.

All of these are, technically speaking, part of the legal system. In essence, they constitute a network of privately negotiated consensual agreements. They enable the middle class to minimize its contact with the legal profession largely because the parties involved have a rough parity of bargaining power—and because, as a last resort, either party usually can threaten to hire a lawyer and utilize all the law's subtlety, delay, refinement, insensitivity and winner-take-all principle to vitiate the worth of victory for either side. Ironically, the poor have been dragged into this system and forced to participate without any parity of bargaining power—and without even the ultimate threat of the middle class: to hire a lawyer and thus compel the supplanting of both parties with professional combatants.

Just as the day of the hired gunman passed when the

homesteaders learned to hire their own mercenaries, so too the rule of law may be about to pass into a new phase once the poor are provided with access to neighborhood law offices. With gunmen on both sides, the irrationality of this mode of conflict resolution may begin to dawn on our society. But if legal services programs for the poor are to make a contribution beyond their own extinction to the emergence of a new system of law for the poor, they must begin to respond to the underlying deficiencies in the legal system with which the middle class has begun to cope, and which private enterprise has long been able to circumvent with considerable success.

Thus, the poor will need their own realtors, their own insurance companies, their own corporate structures, their own arbitration associations, their own administrative tribunals, their own means for entering into private consensual arrangements that reflect their needs and desires with fidelity.[46]

The move towards greater equality requires attention to little evident areas of difference in basic services. These services not only directly affect well-being but also influence the capacity to secure income. A major part of the community action programs of the war on poverty has sought to improve the services available to the poor, either by direct improvements (for example, advances in the social services by instituting multiservice centers accessible to low-income areas) or by encouraging the organization of residents of poverty localities so that they could more effectively demand services. Important strides have been made in getting better and more services into low-income areas, especially black neighborhoods.

But some retrogression also seemed to occur in the late 1960's. The drains of the Vietnam War, the leveling out of the Office of Economic Opportunity budget, and the bitter financial ills of big cities resulted in curtailing important services. The halt in reducing service inequalities may be temporary. If it is, future expansion will make clear that radical reorganization rather than merely increasing scale is necessary. In health care, for example, Medicare and Medicaid have driven up costs as well as increased services. The delivery of "more" leads to fundamental issues of how to organize to produce a useful more. But it is important to recognize that neither "more" nor "better" can be realized without new funds. The new panacea of "coordination" cannot substitute for money.

NOTES

1. On the other hand, the recommendations of the Institute of Economic Affairs and similar groups largely ignore the issue of reductions in inequalities.
2. Martin Rein and S. M. Miller, "Poverty, Policy and Choice" in Leonard Goodman, ed., *Economic Progress and Social Welfare* (New York: Columbia University Press, 1966). A version of this article appears in *Transaction* (September 1967).

3. See S. M. Miller, Pamela Roby and Alwine de Vos van Steenwijk, "Social Policy and the Excluded Man" (New York: New York University, 1968, stencil).
4. See the U.S. Office of Economic Opportunity, *Catalogue of Federal Programs for Individual and Community Improvement* (Washington, D.C.: U.S. Government Printing Office, December 1965), for general eligibility requirements of federal assistance programs.
5. Philip R. Lee, "Health and Well-Being," *The Annals of the American Academy of Political and Social Science,* CCCLXXIII (September 1967).
6. A total of 4.6 physician consultations were made per year by persons with family incomes under $2,000, as compared with 5.7 visits made by those with family incomes over $7,000. Youths under fifteen in families with incomes under $2,000 made 3.0 visits, as compared with 5.7 visits made per year by youths in families with incomes over $7,000. *Over three times as many dental visits* were made per year by persons with incomes over $7,000 as by those with family incomes under $2,000. U.S. Department of Health, Education and Welfare, "Health Status and Family Income: United States," *Vital and Health Statistics; Data from the National Health Survey,* Ser. 10, No. 9 (May 1964); and Charlotte Muller, "Income and the Receipt of Medical Care," *American Journal of Public Health,* LV, No. 4 (April 1965), 514.
7. U.S. Department of Health, Education and Welfare, *op. cit.*
8. Oscar Ornati, *Poverty Amid Affluence* (New York: The Twentieth Century Fund, 1966), p. 75.
9. Odin W. Anderson and Jacob J. Feldman, *Family Medi-*

cal Costs and Voluntary Health Insurance, a Nationwide Survey (New York: McGraw-Hill Book Company, 1956), p. 74; U.S. National Health Survey, "Dental Care Interval and Frequency of Visits, United States, July 1957–June 1959," *Health Statistics from the U.S. National Health Survey,* Ser. B, No. 14 (1960); National Center for Health Statistics, *Volume of Dental Visits, United States July 1963–June 1964,* Public Health Service Publication No. 1000, Ser. 10, No. 23 (1966); Edward A. Suchman and A. Allen Rothman, "The Utilization of Dental Services," *New York State Dental Journal,* XXXI (April 1965), 151–157; A. L. Russell, "Periodontal Disease and Socioeconomic Status in Birmingham, Alabama," *American Journal of Public Health,* L (February 1960), 206–214; S. S. Stahl and A. L. Morris, "Oral Health Conditions among Army Personnel, The Army Engineer Center," *Journal of Periodontology,* XXVI (July 1965), 180–184.

10. Muller, *op. cit.,* p. 517. Cf. Otto M. Reid, Patricia Arnuado, and Aurilla White, "The American Health Care System and the Poor: A Social Organizational Point of View," *Welfare in Review,* VI, No. 6 (November 1968).

11. Muller, *op. cit.,* p. 514.

12. For instance, Carl Greenwald, "Effect of Social and Economic Status upon Dental Caries," *Journal of the American Dental Association,* XXVI (April 1939), 665–676; H. B. McCauley and T. M. Frazier, "Dental Caries and Dental Care Need in Baltimore School Children (1955)," *Journal of Dental Research,* XXXVI (August 1957), 546–551; Louis F. Szwedja, "Observed Differences of Total Caries Experience among White Chil-

dren of Various Socioeconomic Groups," *Public Health Dentistry*, XX (Fall 1960), 59–66.

13. Zachary M. Stadt, Henrik Blum, Glen W. Kent, Eleanor Fletcher, Gladys Keyes, and Lloyd A. Frost, "Socio-economic Status and Dental Caries Experience of 3,911 Five-Year-Old Natives of Contra Costa County, California," *Journal of Public Health Dentistry*, XXVI (1966).

14. U.S. Department of Health, Education and Welfare, *op. cit.*, p. 15.

15. These contrasts are found even after the higher proportion of aged among the lowest-income group are allowed for. U.S. National Health Survey, *Health Statistics*, Ser. B-7, B-8, B-10 (Washington, D.C., 1960).

16. Ornati, *op. cit.*, p. 75.

17. In 1964 the nonwhite infant death rate was 41.1 per 100,000; a level has not been recorded for white infants since 1941. *Transaction*, IV, V (April 1967), 4. The maternal mortality rate among Mississippi Negroes is 15.3 per 10,000 live births, more than six times the national average for whites of 2.5. Elinor Langer, "Who Makes Our Health Policy?" *Physician's Forum* (June 1967).

18. Ronald Freedman, Lolagene C. Coombs, and Judi Friedman, "Social Correlates of Fetal Mortality," *The Milbank Memorial Fund Quarterly*, XLIV (1966), 337. The data are from intensive interviews obtained by the Detroit Area Study of the University of Michigan.

19. Charles Kadushin takes exception with the findings summarized above. He concludes, "The fact is that the lower classes are not more likely than the middle class to have a disease or condition but they do react more

violently to it and are more concerned about it. None-theless, neither sociologists nor public health researchers have for the most part taken proper note of the split between getting sick and reacting to it." Charles Kadushin, "Social Class and the Experience of Ill Health," *Sociological Inquiry*, XXXIV (Winter 1964); and "Health and Social Class," *New Society* (December 24, 1964), p. 10. Aaron Antonovsky challenged Kadushin's analysis in "Social Class and Illness: A Reconsideration," *Sociological Inquiry*, XXXVII (Spring 1967), 311–322; and Kadushin replied in "Social Class And Ill Health: The Need for Further Research. A Reply to Antonovsky," *Sociological Inquiry*, XXXVII (Spring 1967), 323–332. Ronald Miller points out that Kadushin's statistics focus upon the relationship between social class and the contraction of disease rather than "what happens *after* one gets an illness," which Kadushin himself notes "is affected by social class even in a modern social system." Miller observes that more important than the contraction of illness, lower-class individuals are less likely "than upper class individuals to receive adequate medical care or to live a long life." Ronald Miller, "Social Class, Illness, Mortality: Kadushin, Antonovsky, and Sociological Obfuscation" (New York: Department of Sociology, New York University, 1968).

20. Evelyn M. Kitagawa and Philip M. Hauser, "Education and Income Differentials in Mortality, United States, 1960" (Chicago: University of Chicago Population Center, 1967, manuscript). The mortality index for men aged twenty-five to sixty-four with less than five years of schooling was 49 per cent higher than for men with some college; it was 86 per cent higher for men with

family incomes of less than $2,000 than for men with incomes over $10,000. For women the rate was 98 per cent higher for those with less than five years of education than for college alumnae, and 41 per cent higher for those with family incomes less than $2,000 than for those with over $10,000. Because the census definition of income, which was used in the analysis, does not take into account savings and other forms of capital or the income decline which generally occurs prior to death, the authors judge education to be a better indicator of social economic status than income for the purpose of their study.

21. Ornati, *op. cit.*, p. 74; U.S. National Center for Health Statistics, *Periodontal Disease in Adults, U.S. 1960–62*, Public Health Service Publication, No. 1000, Ser. 11, No. 128 (1965).

22. Mata Kouvari Nikias, *Social Factors and the Use of Dental Care under Prepayment* (unpublished Ph.D. dissertation, Joint Committee on Graduate Instruction, School of Public Health, Columbia University, 1967), p. V-12. The data cover the period from January 1, 1958, to September 30, 1964, and pertain to 4,680 members in the Group Health Dental Insurance Plan (New York City) cross-section sample.

23. *Ibid.*, p. V-28.

24. *Ibid.*, p. V-49.

25. *Ibid.*, p. V-45.

26. Gouveneur Ambulatory Care Unit of Beth Israel Hospital in New York's Lower East Side and other agencies in the largest United States cities now employ professionals as well as nonprofessionals who speak many dialects of Chinese as well as Spanish.

27. Langer, *op. cit.*, p. 3.

28. American Dental Association, *Distribution of Dentists in the United States by State, Region, District and County* (Chicago: American Dental Association, 1964). Statistics are for 1963.

29. Within Bolivar County, Mississippi, nearly one-third of the enrolled Head Start children were found to be carrying worms in their intestinal tracts, and about 10 per cent of the children were anemic. Entering the county in 1967 with the intention of providing health care, Tufts University quickly found that the medical needs of the people were only part of their overall physical problems. H. Jack Geiger, "Tufts in Mississippi —The Delta Health Center," *Tufts Medical Alumni Bulletin*, XXV, No. 3 (November 1966), 3–10. Malnutrition during pregnancy and the first year of life were found to have irreversible effects on many children, harming the quality of their teeth, their bone structure, and probably the functioning of their brains. Others suffered continuous sores on their feet from lack of shoes. Richard D. Lyons, "Hunger and Sickness Afflict Mississippi Negro Children," *The New York Times*, March 25, 1968.

30. Muller, *op. cit.*, p. 517. Also see J. Ehrlich, M. A. Morehead, and R. E. Trussell, *The Quantity, Quality and Costs of Medical and Hospital Care Secured by a Sample of Teamster Families in the New York Area,* (New York: Columbia University School of Public Health and Administrative Medicine, 1962); and M. A. Morehead *et al.*, *A Study of the Quality of Hospital Care Secured by a Sample of Teamster Family Members in New York City* (New York: Columbia University School of Public Health and Administrative

114

Medicine, 1964). These studies document how frequently the care received by members of a union through traditional sources proved inadequate. The relationships between quality of care and hospital and physician characteristics are analyzed.

The proportion of consumption and of income going to medical care is relatively high (9.3 per cent) in the lowest-income group, declining to 6.3 per cent at $4,000, staying close to this proportion as income continues to rise. High proportionate expenditure in low-income groups is only partly due to age (sixty-seven was the average age of heads of families with incomes under $1,000.) The average per capita family medical expenditure is $100 for families with incomes below $3,000 and $248 for families with incomes over $15,000 (Muller, *op. cit.*, p. 519). Between 1953 and 1958 the mean gross family expenditure for personal health services increased considerably more among low-income than high-income families. Families with incomes under $2,000 experienced a 27 per cent increase, those with incomes of $2,000 to $3,499 a 49 per cent increase, and those with incomes of $7,500 and over a 16 per cent increase. Odin Anderson, Patricia Collette, and J. J. Feldman, *Changes in Family Medical Care Expenditures and Voluntary Health Service: A Five-Year Resurvey* (London: Oxford University Press, 1963), p. 17.

31. Muller, *op. cit.* While many doctors donate outstanding services to low-income patients or use sliding scales, the share of industrial and philanthropic services in private spending is small—4.5 per cent out of $23.8 billion private expenditure for medical service. Muller, *op. cit.*, p. 512.

32. Alvin Schorr, "Policy Issues in Fighting Poverty," *Children,* XI, No. 4 (July–August 1964), 127–131. This point is made by Brian Abel-Smith in his essay, "Whose Welfare State?" in Norman MacKenzie, ed., *Conviction* (London: MacGibbon & Kee, 1959).

33. *The New York Times,* September 4, 1967, Sec. 1, p. 1. Data from a survey conducted by the J. F. Kraft public opinion organization in Harlem and released by Senator Ribicoff suggest that residents are more concerned about police protection than police brutality. The persons interviewed wanted more instead of fewer police in neighborhoods.

34. Angus Campbell and Howard Schuman, *Racial Attitudes in Fifteen American Cities* (Ann Arbor, Michigan: Survey Research Center, 1968), p. 40.

35. In a random sample of 10,000 households during the summer of 1965, the National Opinion Research Center found that almost 14 per cent of the Negroes, as compared with only 3 per cent of the whites, interviewed responded that the police's respectfulness "toward people like yourself was not so good." Phillip H. Ennis, "Crime Victims and the Police," *Transaction,* IV, No. 7 (June 1967), 42.

36. Patricia Sexton, *Education and Income* (New York: The Viking Press, Inc., 1961), pp. 143–144.

37. Campbell and Schuman, *op. cit.,* p. 40.

38. See Feleks Gross, *The Polish Worker: A Study of a Social Stratum* (New York: Roy Publishing Co., 1945). Cesar Grana notes that when the school children of polyglot New York do visit a museum, they find themselves "the guests of a mansion conceived, not only as a monument to 'values,' but as a re-enactment of the

patrician past." Cesar Grana, "The Private Lives of Public Museums," *Transaction*, IV, No. 5 (1965), 23–24.

39. Dorothy K. Newman, "The Decentralization of Jobs," *Monthly Labor Review* (May 1967). It would cost a worker in Harlem $40 a month to commute by public transportation to work in an aircraft plant in Farmingdale, L.I., in a parts plant in Yonkers or Westchester, or in a basic chemical plant on Staten Island.

40. Project Labor Market, New York University (Oscar Ornati, director), *An Analysis of the Transportation Requirements of Residents of Poverty Areas in New York City Based on a Report by James Whittaker,* January 1968.

41. *Ibid.*, pp. 13–19. Cf. Oscar Ornati, *Transportation Needs of the Poor* (New York: Frederick A. Praeger, 1969).

42. Jerome E. Carlin, *Lawyers' Ethics: A Survey of the New York City Bar* (New York: Russell Sage Foundation, 1966), p. 177. In New York City fewer than 5 per cent of the lawyers report that the median income of their clients is under $5,000 a year, although 50 per cent of the total families and unrelated individuals have incomes under this amount. Conversely, 70 per cent of the lawyers report that the median incomes of their clients is in excess of $10,000, though fewer than 10 per cent of New York's families and unrelated individuals receive incomes that high. See also U.S. Department of Health, Education and Welfare, *Conference of Extension of Legal Services to the Poor,* Jeanette Stats, ed. (Washington, D.C.: U.S. Government Printing Office, 1965).

43. 372 U.S. 335 (1963) and 377 U.S. I (1964).

44. Cf. Jerome E. Carlin and Jan Howard, "Legal Repre-

sentation and Class Justice," *UCLA Law Review,* XII
(January 1965), 432; Jerome E. Carlin, Jan Howard
and Sheldon L. Messinger, "Civil Justice & the Poor,"
Law & Society Review, I, No. 1 (November 1966);
Edgar S. Cahn and Jean C. Cahn, "The War on Poverty:
A Civilian Perspective," *Law Journal,* LXXIII, No. 8
(July 1964); E. Clinton Bamberger, Jr., "The Legal
Services Program of the Office of Economic Oppor-
tunity," William Pincus, "Programs to Supplement Law
Offices for the Poor," and T. F. Broden, Jr., "A Role for
Law Schools in OEO's Legal Services Program," all in
Notre Dame Lawyer, XLI, No. 6, Symposium (1966).

45. J. Skelly Wright, "The Courts Have Failed the Poor,"
The New York Times Magazine (March 9, 1969), p. 26.

46. Edgar S. Cahn and Jean C. Cahn, "What Price Justice:
The Civilian Perspective Revisited," *Notre Dame
Lawyer,* XLI, No. 6, Symposium (1966), 937–938. (The
passage has been editorially reparagraphed by the
authors.)

6
Education and
Social Mobility

The poverty programs of the Economic Opportunity Act of 1964 were largely youth programs; the intent was to break the connection between the situation of low-income parents and the prospects of their children.[1] These programs aimed at increasing the rate of intergenerational social mobility of low-income youth.[2]

More generally, questions of equality and social justice involve issues of social mobility. Life chances are defined largely as questions of opportunity for an individual to rise occupationally in his lifetime or for his children to move into better situations in society, thus surpassing the economic level of their parents. Americans generally point to the educational system to support their ideology that equal opportunity exists for all; the equitable distribution of this education is frequently unquestioned.

Education is increasingly considered the route to social mobility in our credential-oriented society.[3] Because of its consequent importance, we discuss it in this section rather than in the preceding section on basic services. The importance of education is illustrated by the findings of Wilensky and Duncan that it is the only variable which consistently ranks all the white-collar strata above each of the manual and farm strata.[4] In addition to its economic role, educational experience affects the way individuals are treated by other people and by various kinds of organizations and bureaucracies. An individual with low education is an outsider, less able to take advantage of the opportunities that exist, and is treated less well than those with the same income but a higher education. American Negroes' great interest in education, for example, is partially the outgrowth of the protection which education provides against nasty treatment.

Why treat education and social mobility independently? Does not improvement in family income *automatically* result in improvement in chances for social mobility? The data in Fig. 6–1 do not support this conclusion: the education of a family, in most situations, is more important than the income of the family in affecting how far the youth goes in school.[5] Furthermore, two families of the same income obviously fare quite differently in other respects if the offspring of one have a much better chance of higher education and resulting better job prospects than the other. To some extent, then, social mobility is a dimension of well-being deserving of separate attention. It is one of the

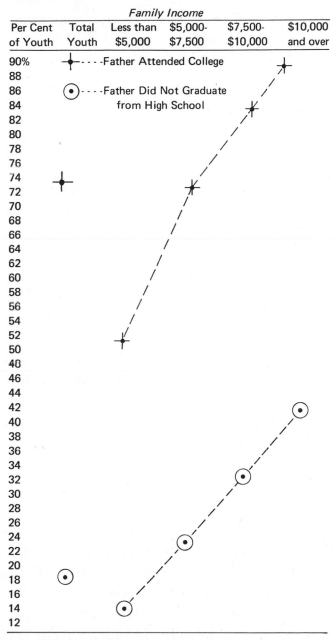

FIGURE 6-1: Percentage of Youth, Age Sixteen to Twenty, Who Were Enrolled in or Attended College in 1960 (by father's education and family income)

		Family Income			
Per Cent of Youth	Total Youth	Less than $5,000	$5,000-$7,500	$7,500-$10,000	$10,000 and over

SOURCE: Pamela Roby, "The Economic Prospects of High School Dropouts, Graduates, and College Graduates," Syracuse University Youth Development Center (1965, mimeo). Adapted from U.S. Bureau of the Census, *Current Population Reports,* Series P-20, No. 110 (July 24, 1961), p. 15, Table 10.

most crucial indicators of a socially democratic society. In this chapter, therefore, we will deal first with education and then with social mobility.

EDUCATION

In education, we may examine various types of indicators of input and output. One input indicator is expenditure data—how much is spent on children of different income levels? The importance of school expenditures is indicated by the finding that the proportion of National Merit finalists is related to a locality's support for education.[6] Data for the city of Chicago in 1963 show that for children in the ten lowest socioeconomic schools, only 63 per cent of the teachers were fully certified; in the ten highest socioeconomic schools the figure was 90 per cent.[7] The significance of this difference is highlighted by Project Talent findings, which show that teacher experience is highly correlated with student achievement. In turn, teacher experience is related to salary.

EXPENDITURES

Despite the growing attention to class differences in education, educational resources are probably not being redistributed in favor of the low-income and the black. The Syracuse University study of school expenditures by Alan Campbell, Jesse Burkhead, Seymour Sachs, and

122

associates shows that in 1962 in thirty-five of the largest metropolitan areas, expenditures in central cities—where there are many low-income children—were $145 per pupil less than in their contiguous suburbs—where there are few low-income children.[8] One of the most disturbing findings in this investigation is that state educational funds give relatively more to the suburbs than to the cities; schools in the suburbs receive $40 more in state aid per pupil than schools in the cities. Even more disconcerting, the gap between cities and suburbs is growing; the difference in 1962 did not exist in 1958, when the two areas were spending the same amount. More recent data are not available but many believe the gaps to be at least as great as in 1962.

Vast regional differences also exist in the distribution of educational resources. Average per pupil expenditures were $413 in Mississippi and $1,125 in New York State during the 1967–1968 school year.[9]

Although many commentators on the Coleman report have focused their attention on data concerning the influence of the family on educational attainment, the report also contains many tables that sharply illustrate the inequities which exist in the distribution of educational resources among America's minority and majority children. Coleman reports:

Nationally, Negro pupils have fewer of some of the facilities that seem most related to academic achievement: They have less access to physics, chemistry, and language laboratories; there are fewer books per pupil in their libraries; their text-

123

books are less often in sufficient supply. To the extent that physical facilities are important to learning, such items appear to be more relevant than some others, such as cafeterias, in which minority groups are at an advantage.

In the metropolitan Midwest . . . the average Negro has 54 pupils per room—probably reflecting considerable frequency of double sessions—compared with 33 per room for whites. Nationally, at the high school level, the average white has 1 teacher for every 22 students and the average Negro has 1 for every 26 students. . . . Secondary school Negro students are less likely to attend schools that are regionally accredited; this is particularly pronounced in the South.[10]

When differences in the quality of the product—the return per dollar of expenditures—are considered, the gap is probably even greater than the gross education figures indicate. It is likely that fewer and poorer services are rendered per dollar in low-income than in higher-income schools. Thus, the gross inequities revealed by the expenditure figures are accentuated by the quality differences.

Table 6–1 indicates that adequate financial aid is probably available to the top 2 per cent of the nation's high school graduates.[11] Even for those who fall within 2 to 10 percentage points from the top in ability, family income is an important determinant of who shall go to college.

After questioning the level and distribution of educational resources, we must also ask, "If we had adequate monetary resources, would we have the capacity to

TABLE 6-1: Percentage of Male High School Graduates Who Entered College within One Year after Completing High School by Aptitude Level and Family Income

Family Income	Aptitude Level (Percentile)				
	0-49.9	50-74.9	75-89.9	90-97.9	98-100
Less than $3,000	19.6	48.2	75.4	87.9	100.0
$3,000-$5,999	27.3	52.5	73.3	86.7	96.1
$6,000-$8,999	31.9	59.7	80.6	88.6	95.2
$9,000-$11,999	40.2	66.8	83.9	92.5	95.9
$12,000 plus	49.7	79.7	90.1	96.7	98.5

SOURCE: U.S. Congress, House, Committee on Education and Labor, Subcommittee on Education, *Hearings*, 88th Cong., 1st and 2nd Sess., 1963-1964.

implement our educational goals in the way we know they should be implemented?" The answer is probably, "No." Not only money, modern school buildings, and technological equipment, such as teaching machines, but *people*—teachers and administrators—are required for effective education. Like so many other things, the capacities of teachers and principals are distributed roughly along a "normal curve." Only a few are very effective; a few are very ineffective; and most are "average." Money that is devoted to new methods of training and guiding teachers and administrators may improve the effectiveness of the poor and average teachers, but it is doubtful whether any technique can make all teachers as effective as those few talented and concerned individuals who stand out as great. These outstanding individuals are the most important educational need of low-income youth in Appalachia, Harlem, or Watts. The need is not easy to fill.

BLACK EDUCATION

Since 1960, young blacks have radically narrowed the education gap that traditionally existed between nonwhites and whites. But the current situation is uneven. Between 1960 and 1968 the difference in median educational attainment of whites and nonwhites twenty-five to twenty-nine years old shrank from 1.9 years to 0.4 years. The difference between the percentage of nonwhites and whites possessing high school diplomas also declined. On the other hand, the gap separating the percentage of whites and nonwhites twenty-five to twenty-nine years old graduating from college increased: the percentage of nonwhites completing college increased from 5.4 per cent in 1960 to 7.7 per cent in 1968, while the numbers of whites doing so increased more rapidly from 11.8 to 15.6 per cent.[12] This gap is significant since the college diploma increasingly separates the "haves" from those who "just get by" in society.

Compounding the educational gap is the disturbing fact that blacks have not reaped the monetary or occupational rewards which education delivers to whites. At every educational level, nonwhites earn less than whites. In 1966, nonwhite college alumni still earned less than white high school dropouts. Between 1958 and 1966, the income gap separating nonwhite and white males with one or more years of college grew from $2,131 to $3,095.[13] A portion of the discrepancy between black and white earnings may be accounted for by differences in the quality of black and white education. Another fraction may be attributed to the higher concentration of blacks working in the South, where wages are low. But discrimination is the only factor which accounts for a major portion of the difference.

Sharp differences exist not only between the earnings but also between the occupational distributions of blacks and whites. Even college graduation does not completely protect blacks from being treated differently than whites in the occupational arena. Differential treatment is experienced at all age levels. In 1964 only 8 per cent of nonwhite high school graduates, as opposed to 30 per cent of white school graduates, sixteen to twenty-one years old who had not enrolled in college, were able to obtain clerical and other white-collar jobs.[14]

At every educational level not only are nonwhites employed in lower-paying, less prestigious occupations than whites, but their chances of obtaining work are also considerably lower than that of whites. In 1968, the unemployment rates were 4.6 per cent for white high school dropouts, as compared with 9.8 per cent for nonwhite high school dropouts; 2.7 per cent for white high school graduates and 6.7 per cent for nonwhite high school graduates; and 1.7 per cent for white college alumni and 2.8 per cent for nonwhite college alumni (age eighteen years and over).[15]

These data indicate that discrimination continues to intervene between education and income, between edu-

127

cation and occupation, and between education and chances for employment. Education is important for the advancement of blacks—we do not wish to be interpreted as arguing otherwise. With education, blacks and other minority groups do gain higher incomes, more prestigious occupations, and a smaller risk of unemployment. The gain is, however, incomplete. The roots of black poverty lie in the discriminatory practices of the larger society as well as their own lack of education. As long as discrimination exists, education alone will not solve the problems of redistributing incomes and occupations between whites and minority members.

Limited Possibilities

Although education is very important, it cannot solve all the problems that produce poverty in American society. "Education" can become a slogan to escape from the wider responsibility of aiding the poor. If educational strategies are not viewed in perspective, an overemphasis on education can be self-defeating, for it may lead to neglect of economic assistance programs. By itself, the educational strategy for poverty reduction suffers from four major limitations: the strategy neglects many poor people; its goals are difficult to achieve, requiring a radical redistribution of resources and first-rate staffs; the strategy is only partially effective for those youths who do obtain education because discrimination and other factors intervene between education and income; its heavy emphasis on education damages individuals and society by constricting alternative channels of occupational mobility and by restricting the pluralism of social values.

By forcing all persons to enter the occupational world through the school gate, we have drastically underestimated and underutilized the potential of many low-income youth. Today nearly one-fourth of white youth and nearly one-half of black youth are dropping or being pushed out of school before they complete high school. In ghetto communities, the proportion is higher. Some of these youths have dropped out because they felt the need to prove themselves "men" by earning money and becoming independent of their parents' small earnings rather than because their schools were "bad."[16] Many youths whose cultures stress the importance of masculinity need alternative routes into the occupational world rather than better schools.

Today dropouts who have gained valuable experience in the work world find that this experience is ignored by employers because the label *dropout*, assigned at age fifteen or sixteen, persists throughout a lifetime. Consequently, individuals who may have outgrown the issues which propelled them out of school continue to be economically disenfranchised. With our increasing emphasis on academic credentials, our Chinese walls of exclusion grow ever higher for persons who are ignored because they lack the magical diploma, although their occupational experience and performance prove them qualified. The loss resulting from an over-emphasis on credentials is society's as well as individuals'.

For education to enrich rather than constrict, men must be free to choose to use or not to use it. It is one of the paradoxes of our time that education, considered to be a liberating force, has become a prison for many. Employers' current emphasis on academic credentials forces individuals to remain in school and makes education a form of coercion; when youths do not follow the schools' mandates, they are sentenced to unemployment, uselessness, and poverty. Until youths are offered alternative entryways to the occupational world, the pressure of *having* to make it through the educational system will continue to be debilitating to many.

Despite the staggering amounts of educational statistics, gaps still exist. Statistics are needed on the distribution of educational resources and quality of education among localities within cities. On the product side, data are needed on the achievement of students. It is important to link expenditures to attainments for specific localities—a need not met in the important National Assessment of Education Program passed by Congress in 1968.[17] Studies of cohorts of students from their entrance into school through maturity would be particularly useful; the objective would be to discern the influences of school performances on their achievements. The absence of such basic information on school outputs is significant. The reluctance of schools to submit themselves to an objective appraisal of some aspects of their performance indicates the possible impact of the availability of such data on pushing schools to change their practices.

SOCIAL MOBILITY

As societies become increasingly future-oriented, a crucial dimension of stratification is what happens to the children of different strata. Current positions of families only partially denote future positions.

Many governmental policies are aimed at reducing the correlation between the economic position of the child and that of his parent. The aim is toward intergenerational social mobility rather than improvement of the conditions of the poor today. In the War on Poverty the emphases on job training programs (for example, Job Corps, Manpower Development) and education (for example, Head Start, Elementary and Secondary Education Act) are essentially programs in social mobility. The programs aimed at the young, such as Head Start, obviously aim toward intergenerational mobility, while those designed for older persons, such as many of the Manpower Development and Training Act programs, seek intragenerational mobility.

What is the value of casting these poverty and manpower programs in the language of intergenerational social mobility? In some cases, the mobility perspective points out that program goals are too low. In some job training programs, for example, success is recorded if the individual secures a job, even if the job pays no more or is no less of a dead end than his previous job.

131

Similarly, low-wage, full-time employment may not be a substantial mobility step over unemployment or irregular employment.

The mobility approach may also indicate the possible importance of stratum or group mobility.[18] Important gains may be achieved not only by moving individuals out of particular low-wage occupations, but by securing a substantial improvement in the relative position in terms of wages, status, and conditions of currently low-level occupations. The large percentage of families living in poverty that are headed by males who are working full time suggests the need for that change. Increasing returns for certain kinds of work may be crucial if poverty is to be rapidly reduced. The stratificational approach also encourages study in the factors which impede or promote mobility. Lack of education may be a less important barrier than current common sense suggests, while discrimination may continue to bar many from jobs or career mobility.[19]

Surprisingly, the United States has lagged behind many other nations in conducting a national study which is mainly addressed to issues of social mobility. In 1962, this lack was remedied by the very useful investigation of the Bureau of the Census, which was stimulated by and conducted in close cooperation with the sociologists Otis Dudley Duncan and Peter Blau. We will use this study. It would be very useful to conduct such a study every five years to record the changes in rates and patterns of social mobility in the United States.

The results of this study show that children of

families at the bottom of the occupational hierarchy have much less chance of moving into upper-level jobs than children who are born in families at these levels. The son of a black manual worker has less than one-fifth the chance of the son of a white-collar non-black to obtain a white-collar job. The white manual worker's son has nearly twice the chance of the black manual worker's son.[20]

The degree of stability of upper-level families is an indication of the openness of society (as well as of economic change and growth). Here, we find downward mobility from the nonmanual into the manual classes to be 22 per cent in the United States, 42 per cent in Great Britain, 37 per cent in Denmark, and 44 per cent in Canada.[21]

In an analysis of the Blau-Duncan data on educational mobility, William Spady found that the differences between men from high and low educational status origins in reaching and completing college appear to be increasing over time in both actual and conditional probabilities.

Although the proportion of sons from the top stratum (college-educated fathers) who reached college increased by over 30 percentage points between the twenties and the fifties, the corresponding percentage among sons from low-status homes (fathers with less than eight years of education) rose less than 6 points. The gap in college graduation also widened, from 22 to 45 per cent. The proportion of sons from low-status homes who finished college has risen imperceptibly while that for sons of college alumni doubled in a period of 40 years.[22]

Since, as James Davis has pointed out, education has a greater effect upon occupation today than ever before, these findings warrant particular concern.[23]

The data on blacks are disturbing. The educational attainments of blacks are consistently lower than those of whites with the fathers' education constant.[24] In addition, the black mobility rate from lower manual occupations is 51 per cent that of whites from these same occupations. More disturbing is the finding that among black sons of higher white-collar fathers, 72.4 per cent fall into manual-occupations, as compared with 23.4 per cent of non-black sons.[25] This rate of downward mobility is spectacular even when we allow for the likelihood that for some the movement may be into manual occupations that pay as well or better than marginal middle-class occupations.

What is the target in social mobility? Obviously, income, occupational and social contacts of families, know-how, and educational support all combine to make it difficult to reduce sharply competitive advantages. But substantial curtailing is possible, and specific targets over a ten- and twenty-year period are probably desirable to reduce social mobility differentials in that time period. The improvement of the education of those at the bottom of society, reduction of the emphasis on educational credentials as intrinsic to occupational entrance, and more effective reliance on up-grading and training on the job are among the ways that social mobility patterns can become political questions. But it is doubtful if high social mobility rates can be produced

134

without a relative improvement in the income of those at the bottom. For the conditions of the family affect the possibilities of the children.

Cutting the link between the parent's position and that of the child is one of the core goals of a fluid society. (One can argue that the goal is to break the link only for those at the bottom, not those in more advantaged positions.) Careful collection and analysis of data of this kind are essential to keeping the issue under public scrutiny.

Obviously, there are important questions concerning the significant economic-political-social boundaries of high and low position. Social stratification analysts have been slow to refine the manual-nonmanual divide. Our conclusion is that the increasingly important social division is not between the manual and nonmanual groups but between those with and without a college diploma—between those in professional and managerial occupations and the rest of society. As Kolko has remarked ". . . economic mobility in a technology and society enormously—and increasingly—dependent on the formally trained expert ultimately reflects the extent of equality in education."[26] Important differences obviously exist below the professional-managerial level, but the expanding "diploma elite" is becoming distinctly advantaged in society.[27] Their advantage is not only economic but social and political as well. The diploma elite manages to achieve deference and decent treatment from governmental organizations and at the same time—perhaps because of this—is able to organize effectively as a political voice. As the complexity of life in the United States increases, we may expect the importance of education to grow.

The increased concern with intergenerational social mobility means that it cannot rest as a residual of other acts in society. What the rate of mobility will be is a political concern today. As such, forceful actions are necessary to affect the patterns and speed of change. Since societies are evaluated on the criterion of mobility, they must move to affect their performance directly rather than permitting general economic and social trends and structures to legislate the future of the young.

The hope has been in the United States that the doors to (educational) opportunity could be flung open without raising the (income) floors of the families of the youth. In the late 1960's, income, rather than opportunity alone, became an issue. In the 1970's, the balance between the two—between directly increasing the income of the disadvantaged and improving the schools —will be of central importance.

NOTES

1. For a discussion of the limitations of the educational strategy for poverty reduction, see S. M. Miller and Pamela Roby, "Education and Redistribution," in Robert L. Greene, ed., *Racial Crisis in American Education* (Chicago: Follett Publishing Company, 1969).

2. A contrasting approach of improving social conditions tends to be family-oriented, more concerned with the aged than youth. These two approaches are discussed in S. M. Miller, "Poverty," in *Proceedings, Sixth World Congress of Sociology* (1967).

3. Cf. S. M. Miller, *Breaking the Credentials Barrier* (New York: The Ford Foundation, 1968). Lenski has written, "Of all the changes linked with industrialization, none has been more important than the revolution in knowledge. . . . From the standpoint of the occupational class system, this development has been highly significant. To begin with, it has been responsible for the considerable growth in size, importance, and affluence of the professional class. Second, it has caused education to become a much more valuable resource, and made educational institutions far more important in the distribution of power and privilege, than ever before in history." Gerhard Lenski, *Power and Privilege* (New York: McGraw-Hill Book Company, 1967), p. 364.

4. O. D. Duncan, "Methodology Issues in the Analysis of Social Mobility," in Neal Smelser and S. M. Lipset, eds., *Social Structure and Mobility in Economic Development* (Chicago: Aldine Publishing Company, 1966); Harold Wilensky, "Class, Class Consciousness and American Workers," in William Haber, ed., *Labor in a Changing America* (New York: Basic Books, Inc., 1966).

5. This finding is partially explained by the University of Michigan's Survey Research Center's report that family income is by no means the major explanatory variable of the amount of money parents spend on their children's higher education. Low-income parents with higher education spend more than poorly educated

higher-income parents. John B. Lansing, Thomas Lorimer, and Chikashi Morigachi, *How People Pay for College* (Ann Arbor, Mich.: Survey Research Center, 1960).

6. Robert C. Nichols, "The Financial Status of National Merit Finalists," *Science,* CXLIX (September 1965), 1071.

7. Urban America, Inc., and The Urban Coalition, *One Year Later* (New York: Frederick A. Praeger, 1969), p. 30.

8. The report is summarized in the *Carnegie Quarterly,* XIV (Fall 1966). The Coleman report on education has same contradictory evidence, but it is highly debatable. The data reported in James Morgan *et al., Income and Welfare in the United States* (New York: McGraw-Hill, 1962), tends to support the general notion of differences in per capita educational expenditures between high- and low-income communities.

9. U.S. Department of Health, Education and Welfare, Office of Education, *Digest of Educational Statistics, 1968* (Washington, D.C.: U.S. Government Printing Office, 1969), p. 61, table 72.

10. James S. Coleman, *Equality of Educational Opportunity* (Washington, D.C.: U.S. Department of Health, Education and Welfare, 1966), pp. 9, 12.

11. Alex Rysman has noted that even this is actually an overly optimistic picture because many of the nation's most talented youth, especially those in the ghetto, are dropped or "pushed" out of school before obtaining the high school diploma. Cf. William H. Sewell and Vimal P. Shah, "Socioeconomic Status, Intelligence, and the Attainment of Higher Education" (Paper for the Re-

search Group on the Sociology of Education at the Seventh World Congress of the International Sociological Association, Evian, France, September 1966).

12. U.S. Department of Health, Education and Welfare, *op. cit.,* p. 9, table 9; U.S. Bureau of the Census, *Current Population Report,* series P-20, No. 182 (April 28, 1969), table 1.

13. U.S. Bureau of the Census, *Current Population Reports,* Series P-60, No. 53 (December 28, 1967), p. 40; and No. 33 (1960), table 26.

14. National Urban League, *Education and Race* (New York: National Urban League, Inc., 1966), p. 16.

15. Elizabeth Waldman, "Educational Attainment of Workers," *Monthly Labor Review* (February 1969), p. 18, table 2.

16. See Patricia Sexton, *The Feminized Male* (New York: Random House, Inc., 1969).

17. The Committee on Assessing the Progress of Education (CAPE) has announced that achievement will be assessed in ten subject-matter areas, beginning with science, citizenship, and writing, during 1969, the first year of a three-year cycle. During the following two years, literature, social studies, music, mathematics, reading, art, and vocational education will be covered. Then the cycle will be repeated. Assessment exercises will be given on a sample basis to students in public, private and parochial schools, as well as to out-of-school seventeen-year-olds and young adults. Data will be released according to the following subdivisions: male and female; four ages (nine, thirteen, seventeen and twenty-five to thirty-five); four geographic regions (northeast, southeast, central and west); type of com-

139

munity (large city, urban fringe, middle-sized city and rural small town; race (white, Negro and other); and two socioeconomic levels (over and under the poverty line). Comparisons between individuals, schools, and school systems will not be made. Committee on Assessing the Progress of Education, *How Much Are Students Learning? Plans for a National Assessment of Education* (Ann Arbor, Mich.: CAPE, 1969).

18. See S. M. Miller, "Comparative Social Mobility," *Current Sociology,* IX, No. 1 (1960).

19. We ignore in this discussion intragenerational mobility; the changes in occupations of an individual over his lifetime; or stratum mobility, the changes in income and other benefits of an occupation compared to other occupations. These are both important processes, which have not been given enough attention in current discussions of mobility. Nor do we discuss geographical mobility, which is frequently, though not necessarily, involved in the patterning of social mobility. We will also ignore the difficulties intrinsic to mobility studies. For this discussion, see S. M. Miller, "Comparative Social Mobility," chap. 1.

20. Otis Dudley Duncan, "Patterns of Occupational Mobility among Negro Men," *Demography,* V, No. 1 (1968), 19, Table 6. The data are for men aged 25 to 64 years and compare fathers' main occupation with the occupation held by sons in 1962.

21. The foreign data are from S. M. Miller, "Comparative Social Mobility." They are for earlier years than the United States figures. But the earlier United States data suggest that there is a significant gap in downward fluidity between the United States and a number of other nations.

22. William G. Spady, "Educational Mobility and Access: Growth and Paradoxes," *American Journal of Sociology,* LXXIII, No. 3 (November 1967), 277.

23. James A. Davis, "Higher Education: Selection and Opportunity," *The School Review,* LXXI, No. 3 (Autumn 1963), 249–265.

24. Spady, *op. cit.,* p. 263.

25. Otis Dudley Duncan, "Patterns of Occupational Mobility among Negro Men." The Negro data indicate the inadequacies of utilizing national figures. Data for regions of the country would probably show that the South has a much lower rate of social mobility than other parts of the country.

26. Gabriel Kolko, *Wealth and Power in America: An Analysis of Social Class and Income Distribution* (New York: Frederick A. Praeger, 1962), p. 113.

27. Cf. S. M. Miller, "Comparative Social Mobility."

7
Power and Powerlessness

POVERTY AS POWERLESSNESS

A poor person is not just a person who is lacking the economic wherewithals—he is also poor if he lacks power. This is a fundamental issue in the whole problem of poverty. Specifically, I would suggest that a Negro who has money, who may be lower middle class in Mississippi, who is denied equity in the courts, denied equal police protection, who has absolutely no representation in his own government, and who can be murdered with impunity by any white man who has nothing more to fear than a possible federal conviction for infringing upon the civil rights of his murdered victim—I would suggest that this man is, in fact, poor.

Saul D. Alinsky, *The Poor and the Powerful*

Not only has the government become a direct dispenser or withholder of resources, as discussed in previous chapters, but it is also regulating, controlling, and di-

142

recting the economy, even in nonsocialist societies. Efforts to spur economic growth and to prevent recessions inevitably involve questions of who is to benefit, who is to pay the costs of trying to keep prices from rising rapidly, who is to be disadvantaged by economic changes? The expanding role of government means that presumed notions of market automaticity succumb to political decisions about who gains and loses.[1] These decisions are supposedly made on immutable technical grounds alone.[2] But, with greater sophistication, these decisions are found to be based upon a political struggle among groups and individuals who possess different values and power.[3]

Consequently, political position becomes increasingly important in affecting the command over resources, and the political dimension of stratification grows in significance. For generations, the arena of action was more narrowly the workplace, the setting of production. Recently, in the United States, low-income persons have been organizing to affect their rights to welfare and other forms of government services rather than to affect the economic market. The relationships to government bureaucracy have become important not only for the poor and discriminated but for all segments of American society.[4] The issues of class and economics are intimately politicized as the marketplace and property are affected by governmental action and political formations. "Black Power" not "Black Wealth" became the mid-1960's rallying cry.

Improvement of economic position does not always bring with it advances in political position.[5] Indeed, many analysts argue that the inconsistency between rising economic power and stunted political power is most likely to make a group revolutionary or militant. A major part of Max Weber's implicit critique of Marx's theory of class stresses the possible disjunctures between economic, social, and political positions.

Historically, efforts toward political advance of the bottommost social groups have emphasized citizenship rights of suffrage. The nineteenth century in Europe witnessed a long, drawn-out struggle for the extension of voting rights to the disenfranchised. By World War I the fight was largely won in most countries that employ the term *democratic*. The formal, legal right to vote is no longer an issue in most countries. The actual use and importance of that right is the more important question today, with the disturbing exception of Negroes in the American South who still suffer from concerted efforts to limit their voting.

As Richard Scammon's data show, the frequency of voting decreases with income. Some would argue, as may be inferred from Berelson,[6] that it is desirable to have a low voting rate among low-income and low-educated persons because they are likely to be ill-informed, antidemocratic voters. However, the general sentiment defines democracy in part as the integration of low-income persons into the political process.

What should be the target for voting in the low-income group? No group has 100 per cent voting rates. The voting rate for higher-income groups (incomes of $10,000 and more) is 84.9 per cent; this contrasts with 57.6 per cent in the group in the $2,000 to $2,999 range

144

and 49.6 per cent in the low-income range (below $2,000).[7] The largest jump in voting rates is between the $3,000 to $4,999 group and the $5,000 to $7,499 group; the former rate is 62.7 per cent, and the latter is 72.4 per cent. This latter figure might well serve as the goal for voting rates among the low income.[8]

To achieve this level would require not only the elimination of the de facto resistances to black voting but the reduction of the varied requirements that limit voting: residence requirements, English literacy, loss of voting rights because of imprisonment.[9] Increasing the ease of voting may also be necessary: more polling places, longer polling hours, elimination of registration so that only one visit is needed in order to vote.[10] A third barrier to voting is, of course, a lack of interest in voting and the political process, which is caused by apathy or a feeling that the issues and candidates are not important or do not involve a significant choice.

The implicit notion here is that low voting rates among low-income persons who have been discriminated against should not be regarded as merely a defect in the nonvoters but as a criticism of the political process.

REPRESENTATION

Voting is but one aspect of the issue of political rights. Another is the importance of the vote, which leads to the question underlying the agitation about reappor-

145

tionment: Are voters in different areas securing equal representation in a legislative body, whether it be Congress, a state assembly, or a city council? At another, more subtle level, the question is: Do the representatives of the low-income group have as much sensitivity to their interests and wishes as the representatives of higher-income groups? The indicators of these conditions are difficult but not impossible and are best developed and maintained by nongovernmental groups. The simplest indicator is the AFL-CIO report on the voting records of congressmen and senators on key labor issues. The main issues (and positions) for low-income individuals could be delineated,[11] and representatives from low-income districts could be rated on the positions they took on these issues; this could be done by civil rights and poverty groups. If similar measures were maintained for higher-income groups, it would be possible to ascertain whether large differences exist in the sensitivity of representatives of different socioeconomic groups.[12] It would seem "natural" for civil rights groups and poverty-oriented groups, such as the Center for Community Change, to maintain such indexes.

The concept of *sensitivity of representatives* perhaps begs the question because frequently the legislative decisions are not of deep significance to low-income voters. If the issues are marginally important, then the sensitivity of the representatives is not crucial. Radical critics raise the question of whether the overlap of the two main parties buries critical issues of redistribution

146

since they both endeavor to appeal to a Nixon-heralded voter in the center. From the point of view of the low-income group, to what extent are the issues that come before legislative bodies of central importance? Are gaping needs left untouched? Obviously, a mode of analysis along these lines is exceedingly difficult and could best be pursued outside of government.

Indeed, except for voting rates, most appraisals of performance in the political realm should be conducted by independent groups, not only because of the strong repercussions of the results and the likelihood that they may be manipulated for partisan purposes, but, more importantly, because competing indicators and interpretations are desirable. Different groups and interests need quite different sets of information and interpret them in very contrasting ways.

BUREAUCRACY

Our analysis so far has been focused on level of voting and representation. However, the administration as well as the formulation of policy greatly affects political position. The militant attacks on "the welfare state" are partially sparked by concerns about administrative injustices and inhumanity. A modern view of political process and power must analyze the relationships of individuals to nongovernmental as well as to governmental bureaucracies.[13] The proliferation of governmental agencies means that much of what affects the

147

life of the poor emanates from bureaucratic sources. Important decisions are made in administration as well as by legislation. The way in which low-income persons are treated by agency officials may be more important than the laws which these officials purport to administer.

The quality of treatment is the first important aspect of bureaucratic functioning to be considered. Recently the issue of decency in behavior of officials toward citizen-clients has been raised most sharply in the realm of public welfare; there have been charges of invasion of privacy (checking homes in midnight raids to see if there is evasion of the "no-man-in-the-home" rule, now declared unconstitutional by the Supreme Court), utilization of welfare as a means of social control, and general humiliation of clients by welfare officials.[14]

Where aid (money and services) is provided to the poor, their claim to this aid is frequently ambiguous. Do they have rights as citizens to these services, or are they dependents who lose the privilege of rights because of their dependent status? Increasingly, the issue is raised that the provision of cash and services becomes an individual right. If an individual is refused aid, he can appeal if necessary to an adjudicating body that is independent of the agency. If he is poorly treated, he can protest and demand to have the official punished. (The example of police review boards leaps into mind even though scarce in practice.)

The second important aspect of bureaucratic functioning that must be considered is the extent to which programs contain statements of rights that are useful and effective. How are individuals protected against control by bureaucratic agencies? Does an agency have a grievance procedure which meets the criteria of effectiveness (labor union history with grievance procedures would probably offer many ways of evaluating procedures)? If so, who uses it, on what issues, and with what results? The ability to be relatively insulated against bureaucratic mishandling and injustice is differentially distributed in society—higher-income and better-educated persons manage more effectively than low-income and low-educated persons.[15]

A third aspect of bureaucratic functioning concerns the issue of pluralism. In a *pluralistic society* the interests of individuals are represented by organizations and associations. To what extent is the pluralism of American society democratic? Do low-income groups have effective voices? How involved are they in the discussions of their groups? What changes are taking place? To what extent are political processes being transformed so that recipients of governmental benefits become consumers and citizens with a decision-making role rather than dependents without choice or any degree of sovereignty?

Several studies show that "membership in voluntary associations increases with status, and that membership in associations increases interest in Presidential elections."[16] Gradations within the low-income strata are important. In a study of New York City poor, David Caplovitz found that, for the sample as a whole and within each racial group, the more solvent families more often belonged to voluntary associations.[17] This finding suggests that the relationship between voluntary-association membership, voting, and social class found in the general population "occurs within the lower class as well; the less the financial stability of the low income family, the less its participation in the life of the broader community."

PARTICIPATION

Quality of treatment, rights, and grievance representation are important issues; they are inadequately supplied by bureaucracies today. However, a new demand has emerged, which is insufficiently represented in indicators of these types. This fourth issue has been dramatically and ambiguously phrased as *maximum feasible participation*—the right to share in the decision-making of administrative agencies.[18] Since so many important decisions are made outside the realm of the legislature, administrative law-making and allocations become increasingly important. While the demand for participation is multifaceted—many supported it initially because it reduces the psychological feeling of powerlessness—in this context, participation is clearly a political act of involvement in important decisions which are nonlegislative. The Office of Economic Opportunity is experimenting with indicators of grass-roots involvement in local community-action programs; hope-

150

fully, these indicators may be adapted to broader use since the issues of participation are much broader than poverty programs.

During the early 1960's, Almond and Verba developed more sensitive indicators of participation. When they asked United States, British, German, Italian and Mexican citizens whether they had ever attempted to influence the local government or the national legislature, followed accounts of political affairs, paid attention to campaigns, sometimes discussed politics, belonged to volunteer associations or belonged to volunteer associations involved in politics, they found that the United States respondents were on the average considerably higher on every account than the other respondents. Although, as Verba points out, the United States figures are higher than those of other nations, the figures within the United States are disturbing because marked differences exist between black and white participation rates. In the United States finding, no difference exists in black and white participation in associations involved in politics, and little difference exists in the amount of attention blacks and whites report paying to politics, but whites, considerably more than blacks, attempt to influence local and national government. Verba suggests that this finding indicates that blacks are as "ready" in terms of organization and interest as whites to participate—but must overcome other barriers before being able to do so.[19]

The new politics will increasingly involve the relationships of citizens to the apparatus of the welfare

151

state. While the participation issue has begun to be raised in terms of the poor, increasingly it will be raised for other groups in society. The issue of the welfare state is most acute for the poor but affects other citizens as well. It may be that the call for political participation in decision-making on a wider scale is not a call for reduction of inequalities since higher-income citizens also have limited participation. But the losses of these citizens owing to inadequate participation in decision-making may be less important to them than the losses of the poor who are so deeply affected by bureaucratic practices. Refinements of measures of powerlessness are needed.

A fifth aspect of bureaucratic functioning concerns the psychological feeling of powerlessness.[20] The poor feel less able to control their destinies than do other groups in society. "The government," "they," "city hall" loom large, threatening and immovable to many of the poor. Changes in the feeling of powerlessness would not only affect their willingness to vote, to make changes and participate in decision-making, but may also be important in contributing to an important state of well-being. Indicators of changes in feelings of powerlessness could be constructed on the basis of the studies of alienation and anomie (indeed, they have been involved in some evaluations of poverty programs). Public-opinion surveys could provide relevant data on the indicators. Some institutions may appear to be more permeable than others, and indicators of feelings concerning particular institutions may be necessary.

As with all subjective indicators, the danger of manipulation is important: policies may successfully aim at making people feel more politically powerful even though their political potence has not grown. Here, again, it would be important for nongovernmental groups to gauge independently the realistic significance of changed feelings of powerlessness (also, the converse may occur—increased political control without decreased feelings of powerlessness).

WORKPLACE

We have discussed power in the political realm, at the federal, state, local or bureaucratic organizational levels. As Ralf Dahrendorf has asserted, "class is about power."[21] The conflict over authority is the universal issue, of which the Marxist concern with property is a special, though important, case.[22]

We have not discussed power and authority relationships in the workplace—a sixth dimension of power. The jobs of the poor are less frequently rationalized than the jobs of higher-income groups; they are less frequently organized into unions; low-skill workers are more easily replaceable than high-skilled workers, so that employers can be more forceful with the former group (or so it would seem). Indicators of workplace independence and participation would be useful, for the nature of job authority is an important part of well-being even if it is not fully recognized as such today.[23]

We suspect that in the future discussions of democracy in the political process will be supplemented by reopening questions about authority at work, although not necessarily in the traditional forms of socialist ownership or shibboleths of worker participation.[24]

The 1960's opened on a self-congratulatory note of the "end of ideology" which implied consensus on values and means and made possible "the professionalization of reform." It ended in anger, discontent, and disagreement. The most revolutionary dissenters did not even offer a program or a vision; rather they wished "to tear down the structure." Whatever else this outlook means, it conveys sharp feelings about power, its character, distribution, and accountability in American society. For what is being asserted is many citizens' feeling of low participation and ineffectiveness in affecting key decisions.

Black and other minority groups in this society have tied their psychological as well as their material well-being to the development of something amorphously called "power." "Black power" is paralleled by "Brown power" among Mexican Americans and "Red power" among Indians. It is unclear where this power concern will go. But what is definite is the insistence that, for the poor and the discriminated, the political dimension is of enormous importance. In the struggle to reduce inequality (and to widen democracy for all, not just the less equal), new institutions will be constructed and old institutions restructured, sometimes in anticipation of the pressure and need for change, more frequently in reluctant capitulation to little understood demands.

NOTES

1. See the important discussion of citizenship in T. Marshall, *Class, Citizenship and Social Development* (New York: Doubleday & Co., Inc., 1963). When describing nineteenth- and twentieth-century European changes in citizenship, Dahrendorf has stated, "The slogan (political participation) points to a symptom of the development of equality of citizenship rights rather than to its entire substance. Citizenship is the social institution of the notion that all men are born equal. Its establishment requires changes in virtually every sphere of social structure. Apart from universal suffrage, equality before the law is as much a part of this process as is universal education, protection from unemployment, injury and sickness, and care for the old. Representative government, the rule of law, and the welfare state are in fact the three conditions of what I should describe as the social miracle of the emergence of the many to the light of full social and political participation." Ralf Dahrendorf, "Recent Changes in the Class Structure of European Societies," *Daedalus,* XCIII (Winter 1964), 239.

2. Cf. Martin Rein and S. M. Miller, "Poverty Programs and Policy Priorities," *Transaction,* IV, No. 9 (September 1967).

3. For a strong attack on the "assertion that the old sources

of tensions and class conflict are being progressively eliminated or rendered irrelevant . . .," see J. H. Westergarrd, "Capitalism without Classes?" *New Left Review*, No. 26 (Summer 1964), pp. 10–32. Also pertinent to these issues is John H. Goldthorpe's essay, "Social Stratification in Industrial Society," in Reinhard Bendix and S. M. Lipset, eds., *Class, Status, and Power* (New York: The Free Press, 1966), pp. 648–659.

4. Dahrendorf links class and politics even more closely when he writes, "class is about power and power is about politics." Dahrendorf, *op cit*. While class and power are closely related, we also believe that for conceptual purposes they have to be independently analyzed.

5. Janowitz and Segal note that in Great Britain, Germany, and the United States "there is a tendency for persons in the lower working classes to have a higher degree of non-party affiliation than in the other strata of society." However, they note that the source of ineffective political participation lies not in income and education per se, but "as a series of life experiences which produces persons . . . without adequate institutional links to the political system." Furthermore, ". . . such disruption can occur at various points in the social structure, for example among elderly men and women living outside family units." Morris Janowitz and David R. Segal, "Social Cleavage and Party Affiliation: Germany, Great Britain and the United States," *American Journal of Sociology*, LXXII, No. 6 (May 1967).

6. Bernard Berelson, Paul F. Lazarsfeld, and W. N. McPhee, *Voting* (Chicago: The University of Chicago Press, 1954).

7. Richard M. Scammon, "Electoral Participation," *The Annals of the American Academy of Political and Social Science*, CCCLXXI (May 1967), 63.

8. Here, as elsewhere in this book, we are not discussing the inequalities which affect other than the low income. In the case of youth, the obvious point is the issue of the lowering of the voting age to eighteen.

9. David Caplovitz and other students of Harlem voting patterns contend when adjustments are made for non-eligibles, the voting rate in this locality is as high as in high-income neighborhoods. If this is so, increasing ease of voting is not important.

10. Kelley *et al.* found in a sample of 104 cities that 78 per cent of the variation in the percentage of the population of voting age that voted could be accounted for by variations in the percentage of the population of voting age that was registered to vote. Kelley and Gosnell both found a strong relationship between the date at which registration rolls are closed and the percentage of the voting age population which was registered. Stanley Kelley, Jr., Richard E. Ayres, William G. Bowen, "Registration and Voting. Putting First Things First," *American Political Science Review*, LXI, No. 2 (June 1967). Cf. Donald R. Matthews and James W. Prothro, "Social and Economic Factors and Negro Voter Registration in the South," *American Political Science Review*, LVII (March 1963), 24–44; Harold F. Gosnell, *Getting Out the Vote* (Chicago: The University of Chicago Press, 1927); Charles E. Merriam and H. F. Gosnell, *Non-Voting: Causes and Methods of Control* (Chicago: The University of Chicago Press, 1924).

11. What is the needed response on a particular issue from the point of view of a particular socioeconomic grouping is not undebatable. But there would be a high degree of agreement on most issues whether by a panel of experts thinking in terms of a particular group or by a sample of the group itself. At least, this is a testable proposition.

12. Since most voting districts are not homogeneous (and the larger the district, the greater the heterogeneity), a representative would have to be rated in terms of his sensitivity to a particular group rather than to the district as a whole. A less direct way of measuring sensitivity is the MacRae method of seeing to what extent a district is a potential swing district. The higher the potential, the greater the sensitivity of the representatives. Are low-income districts more likely than high-income districts to favor overwhelmingly one candidate or party so that a representative feels little pressure for responding to his constituents' needs and feelings?

13. Parsons suggests that it is useful to conceive of political power more broadly than usual: "Essential as government is, it does not stand alone in implementing major political changes." For example, "the political problems of integration involve all fields of organizational decision-making, especially for business firms to accept Negroes in employment, for colleges and universities to admit them for study, for trade unions to avoid discrimination." Talcott Parsons, "Full Citizenship for the Negro American?" *Daedalus*, XCIV, No. 4 (Fall 1965).

14. After a four-year court battle, Alameda County, Calif., awarded $23,000 in back pay to a social welfare worker who was fired for refusing to participate in the welfare

department's "operation bed-check." It is less likely that the female welfare recipients whose homes were invaded by welfare workers without search warrants will be recompensed. *Berkeley Barb,* V (August 24, 1967), 7.

15. See Charles A. Reich, "Individual Rights and Social Welfare: The Emerging Legal Issues," *The Yale Law Journal,* LXXIV, No. 7 (June 1965).

16. Charles R. Wright and Herbert H. Hyman, "Voluntary Association Memberships of American Adults: Evidence from National Sample Surveys," *American Sociological Review,* XXIII (1958).

17. David Caplovitz, *The Poor Pay More* (New York: The Free Press, 1963), pp. 133–134.

18. See Martin Rein and S. M. Miller, "Participation, Poverty, and Administration," *Public Administration Review,* XXIX, No. 1 (January 1969).

19. Gabriel A. Almond and Sidney Verba, *The Civic Culture* (Princeton, N.J.: Princeton University Press, 1963). For an excellent discussion of participation see Sidney Verba, "Democratic Participation," *The Annals of the American Academy of Political and Social Science,* CCCLXXIII (September 1967), 53–78.

20. Melvin Seeman, "On the Meaning of Alienation," *American Sociological Review,* XXIV (1959), 783–791. Seeman identifies five alternative meanings of alienation: powerlessness, meaninglessness, normlessness, isolation, and self-estrangement. Blauner demonstrates that because the conditions of work and existence in various industrial environments are quite different, the industry the man works in is fateful in furthering or abating each of the five dimensions of alienation expressed by See-

159

man. Robert Blauner, *Alienation and Freedom: The Factory Worker and His Industry* (Chicago: The University of Chicago Press, 1964).

21. Dahrendorf, *op. cit.*
22. Ralf Dahrendorf, *Class and Class Conflict in Industrial Society* (Stanford, Calif.: Stanford University Press, 1959).
23. Blauner has reported the wide variations of responsibility and freedom among blue-collar jobs. He has reopened a number of important issues. Blauner, *op. cit.*
24. Worker participation and control have reemerged as issues in Great Britain. See Ken Coates and Tony Topham, *The Labour Party's Plans for Industrial Democracy*, Pamphlet Series No. 4 (Nottingham, England: Institute for Workers' Control) and other publications by that Institute. The Yugoslav and German experiences are also relevant. On the other hand, General de Gaulle's concern with participation did not seem to win him support.

160

8
Status and Satisfaction

Max Weber's discussion of the status dimension of stratification frequently has been compressed into an analysis of family or occupational-prestige rankings. This reduction is an inadequate rendering of what was obviously intended to embrace the sociopsychological dimensions of stratificational systems.

Three dimensions are worth distinguishing here: social honor, styles of life, and self-respect.

SOCIAL HONOR

In Weber's usage, *social honor* refers to the social evaluation by others of a class or political group. The views that others hold of an individual affect the way that he is treated—with approval or with disapprobation. The "two nations" of Disraeli and Harrington, the "haves" and the "have-nots," are divided not only by income and hope, but by social honor as well.

Social honor is *externally* awarded on a variety of bases: income, occupation, education, family history. In the past, American sociologists overstressed the significance of social prestige and understressed the importance of economic class, but prestige is again growing in importance as a dimension of stratification. Being included in society, which means being accorded respect and accepted in social and political relations with others, is increasingly an important part of the issue of inequality.[1]

The widespread view is that the social gulf between the haves and have-nots has been reduced. Probably a more accurate view is that more individuals are now haves and are acceptable. What about those who are left behind as most men generally advance? Are the lagging less likely now to be viewed as subhuman, undeserving of attention? There probably has been a growth in feelings of humanity, but there still is a sizable difference in the way that low-income and other marginal persons, as compared with higher income "majority" persons, are regarded.

The United States no longer has a legal basis for dishonor in the form of laws that require discriminating against minority groups. However, practices of discrimination frequently exist—on the job, in housing, in public facilities, and in education. Data for overt discrimination are difficult to collect. Crucial activities and localities could be studied, however, to record changes in discrimination patterns and frequency. National cross sections of minority-group members could be studied over a period of time (preferably as a panel) to see whether they have changing experiences with discrimination. In the case of discrimination, the goal is clear-cut: the total elimination of discrimination on the basis of race, religion, ethnic extraction, and income.

Discrimination is the most striking example of a status barrier, but it is not the main dimension of stratification today. The more important dimensions surround the prestige of various groupings in society and the nature of the interactions among groups. Data are lacking on the way that low-income groups are rated by others. The most common data available are those on occupational prestige; they uniformly show that the occupations held by low-income persons are lowest in prestige. In 1947 and 1963, in nationwide samples janitors, bartenders, share croppers, garbage collectors, street sweepers, and shoe shiners ranked among the bottom ten of ninety occupations according to prestige.[2]

What is the goal in reducing prestige differences?[3] We do not anticipate complete equality here but some reduction in the range of differences. Should the goal be random sorting of interaction so that individuals of high income (or education) are as likely to associate with individuals of low income as with their income peers? Should the goal be that ethnic group members will associate no more frequently with fellow ethnics than with nonethnics? Many would argue for ethnic solidarity—at least for political purposes—among deprived groups, such as the blacks. Although we lack clarity as to the goals for a society that (in rhetoric,

163

at least) is pictured as socially democratic, information on these patterns over a period of time would still be useful in depicting the extent to which gulfs between groups are being narrowed.

Interestingly, in this area of contact—social distance and social honor—we have the greatest difficulty in specifying targets. In this sensitive area, the cloudy, ambiguous slogans of American values and goals provide little direction. A more systematic collection of the kinds of information suggested here may force reexamination of broad global tenets and specific behaviors which are poorly articulated and understood.

Because social honor significantly affects government policy, its importance increases with the growing importance of government action that affects persons' well-being and command over resources. For example, a group that is regarded as an *undeserving poor* is much less likely to be aided than a *deserving poor*. Prestige, then, is intimately tied to access to resources. Also, as we shall discuss later, it affects self-respect.

In the United States the issue of desegregation, especially in housing, also points up the significance of prestige. Undoubtedly, much of the slowness in making it possible for blacks to have effective free choice in housing locations is caused by class feelings—disturbance about "lower-class" black families. Nonetheless, a considerable part of the resistance against black mobility is directed against blacks as a status group, regardless of class levels.

The basis for and the way that one receives income

affect the satisfactions derived from income, as noted above. In American society, income that is not obtained directly or indirectly from work or education (for example, scholarships) is likely to be demeaned. Public assistance, which has demeaning means tests, is the major type of transfer payment received by low-income families.

Transfer payments to upper-income groups, on the contrary, generally have the seal of social acceptance. Social security, government payments to farmers, and indirect subsidies in the form of tax deductions, allowances, and exemptions are generally accepted forms of government transfers.[4] In 1963 55 per cent of the total government payments to farmers were accorded to the top 11 per cent of all farmers, that is, those with farm sales of $20,000 and over.[5]

Many of the discussions of the reform of the welfare system are concerned with the importance of removing the stigma associated with receiving income through demeaning tests and eliminating long periods of waiting in noisy, overcrowded, and physically undesirable places. The concern is largely, though not exclusively, with the degradation of the means-test ceremonials.

Cities have begun to respond to these concerns with various experimental reforms. In 1967 the New York City Department of Welfare began experimental application and certification procedures in two of its thirty-three welfare centers. Traditional procedures require an applicant not only to provide documentation in support of his claims for welfare, but to undergo a "field investigation." In contrast, in the experimental centers an applicant signs a special declaration form and without verification, except under special circumstances, his application is either accepted or rejected at the intake interview. The intention of the new procedures is to eliminate many demeaning aspects of the application process, speed application procedures, and free caseworkers from their investigatory functions so that they may spend more time on planning and providing services.[6]

Although in New York City demeaning questioning and probing appear to have been reduced by these experimental procedures, a certain amount still persists. Goldman reports that in the experimental centers, ". . . the use of caseworkers as intake staff appears to foster a situation in which there is an undue concern with past patterns of behavior and an excessive exploration of background issues during the determination of eligibility. . . . Many workers have been unable to accept the use of the Declaration as the sole basis for deciding eligibility. They feel that it is their responsibility to 'catch' applicants who may not be truly eligible."[7] Recommendations have been made to change this situation.

In Trenton, New Jersey, the impact of a widely discussed alternative to the public welfare system, the guaranteed annual income, is being tested for the first time in the United States. The experiment, begun in September, 1968 and involving 800 families, is testing seven separate negative-tax schemes which differ in amounts of payments. The only rigid requirement for the payments, which are based on family income and size, is that the recipients must file an accurate monthly report on earnings and number of dependents.[8] The Nixon Administration is proposing reforms which would substitute the respected Social Security Administration for the calumnized welfare administrations.

In effect, then, we are in the midst of a *politicalization of status,* where the distribution of stigma through the provision of income and services is being challenged. Stigma is now a political issue; the demand is for mechanisms, such as the New York Welfare Declaration Centers, the negative income tax, welfare rights, and family allowances, which reduce the possibilities of families having low status because of the way their income is procured.

STYLES OF LIFE

By *styles of life,* the second dimension of status, we refer to the norms and values of particular groups.[9] If social honor is the way the group is regarded from without, styles of life refer to the way the group behaves. Obviously, styles of life and their interpretation affect the bestowal of social honor.[10]

The determination of styles of life is no easy matter; it is difficult to obtain a summation of a style that is not judgmental, and even more difficult to obtain a style description that does not run afoul of competing efforts

167

to utilize that description in the struggle for policy choices. The significance of styles of life underscores the importance of status considerations in government decisions as well as the importance of government decisions.

Because of the importance of styles of life in affecting social honor and public policy, social science becomes particularly political. Its mode of interpretation has strong reverberations. Yet, the knowledge from which descriptions and interpretations are made is limited and controversial. In an important sense, however, this has always been true; the interpretation of the social stratification of a nation is always a very sensitive political issue. What is striking today is the particular importance of styles of life. The greater controversy surrounding life styles may be attributed to not only the fact of greater stakes (government is more likely to do something now than in the nineteenth century), but also to the production of a larger number of fairly independent social scientists and the politicalization of issues which provide once-neglected groups with spokesmen.

Current research on the poor is leading to the rejection of the notion of the one style of life among this group.[11] It is always difficult to make a historical statement since much of the past is sentimentalized in the telling, but it does appear that life-style heterogeneity within a particular group is indeed increasing. One reason for this is the greater variety of cross pressures that exist today in societies which are increasingly national, where more styles are visible through travel, mass media and television, and where life is more public.

A second reason underlines the mode of stratificational analysis proposed by Weber: change in one dimension of life does not automatically produce change in other realms. Discontinuities often result from a rapid pace of change in which spurts and lags are pronounced.

The heterogeneity of styles is important in two ways. One has been referred to already: the receptivity to aiding particular groups, and especially the poor, depends to a large extent on their social honor. In turn, their social honor depends largely on what purports to be their life styles. Those low-income groups with more appealing life styles are much more likely to be given aid.

Heterogeneity is also important because any given policy is likely to fit more easily into the style and condition of one section of the poor than another. Frequently (whether intended or not) this results in the process of "creaming," that is, working with the poor who are better-off or most adaptable. It usually takes some time to discover that a certain policy leaves behind poor groups with other life styles or other class positions. The process of "creaming" raises the question whether groups need to change their life styles in order to be able to take advantage of new opportunities in the private market or in governmental policies. Here, styles of life become a problematic of the efficacy of change rather than moral gatekeepers determining whether or not a particular group should be helped. People are regarded as more flexible than programs.

Frequently, in the United States, life styles are discussed in terms of relatively impenetrable barriers, which are placed in the way of advance by the culture or subculture of poverty. An alternative formulation, which Riessman and Miller have attempted to develop, emphasizes those aspects of low-income life styles which must be considered in order to make public policies more effective.[12] The stress is on reducing the strains, obstacles, and difficulties of policies rather than on castigating the poor or ignoring their particular outlook.

In a sense, what is important about the styles of life of particular groups, especially those most needful of governmental aid, is largely determined by the political culture of a nation. Whether the bases of life styles are ethnic or marginal economic circumstances, what is crucial about them is the way they interact with political values concerning who should be helped, how they should be helped, and how the behaviors of those helped should change. The style-of-life variable has become more highly charged than it was for Malthus.

SELF-RESPECT

Self-respect, the third dimension of status, concerns the way in which a group regards itself. It is a complex mixture of economic and political conditions, social honor, and styles of life.

170

In contrast to the view of the poor as good savages, healthy and free, most indicators show that they enjoy life less than other groups. As one would expect in an industrial, instrumentally oriented society, the available data are largely about job satisfaction and morale. Here, the results are almost all in the same direction: the higher the job level, the greater the degree of job satisfaction. For example, only 16 per cent of unskilled automotive workers, as compared with over 90 per cent of mathematicians and urban university professors, reported that they would try to get into a similar type of work if they could start all over again.[13]

According to the findings of Bradburn and Caplovitz in their study on happiness, job dissatisfaction is an instance of relative deprivation. Men of low socioeconomic status in prosperous communities were found to be more dissatisfied with their jobs than men of similar circumstances in depressed communities.[14]

Studies of mental health report that the highest rate of severe illness occurs among the lowest socioeconomic groups. For example, in the most famous survey,[15] class V, the bottom group, had a schizophrenic rate of 895 per 100,000, while class I–II had a rate of 111. Unfortunately, as in most studies, this investigation is marred by the possibility of underenumerating illnesses in the upper-income groups. More complex assessments of mental health show that the bottommost class in society is characterized by more emotional instability than higher classes.[16] As a goal, the gross reduction of mental illness, especially severe mental illness, among lower socioeconomic groups would be important; another goal would be to reduce the rates of mental illness in the lower groups as rapidly as they are reduced in the higher groups.

The importance of dignity, satisfaction, self-respect, and self-image is evidenced in the recent movement of the blacks, calling for institutional settings which foster the development of positive self-images. While in part this demand is clearly political in terms of power, at another level it is a psychologically based demand, which insists that the development among blacks of positive attitudes toward themselves is a responsibility of society. While one can argue about the best way to do this—whether "Black Power" and separate institutions are the only instruments—the intent of the goal, positive self-image, is one which many would accept as a societal obligation. *The differential distribution of positive feelings about oneself is perhaps the essence of inequality.*

Recently, studies have been aimed at the elusive issue of happiness.[17] These studies, which form the base for the development of time-series investigations of the nation's psychological well-being, indicate that positive and negative feelings vary independently of each other. Happiness is not the absence of unhappiness. Again, the interrelationships between education and income are complex. Education and happiness are positively related for those who earn less than $7,000 a year but are negatively related among wealthier people.[18]

The Bradburn-Caplovitz study of happiness in four medium-sized communities demonstrates the importance of many items which are not included in the definition of an "adequate level of income." Going for a ride in a car, as well as eating in a restaurant several times a week and participating in or watching games or sports activities, are related to positive feelings. The degree of a community's economic depression is reflected in the happiness of lower but not higher socioeconomic groups. However, economic privation through loss of a job, low income, or increased vulnerability to economic stress with increasing age were found to affect the feelings of individuals more greatly.[19]

In addition to statistical data on actual inequalities, indicators are needed of the perceptions and attitudes toward inequalities in each dimension of well-being: incomes, assets, basic services, social mobility, education, political position, and status. How people perceive of their situation affects their well-being. In England, W. G. Runciman has demonstrated the extent to which attitudes toward social inequalities have failed to correspond with the facts of inequality, whether they be economic, social, or political.[20]

These are difficult issues to discuss in the context of policies without sounding 1984-ish, but the dangers of their manipulation should not prevent us from first exploring some issues even if, on civil-libertarian or democratic grounds, we later decide that we do not wish to pursue study and action along these lines. The

dangers should not obscure the recognition of the ultimate objectives, nor should the seeming neutrality of
the material elements of well-being lead us into taking
easy measurements which eliminate study of the new
demands that are being made of the affluent society.
For example, in the kibbutz, it has been reported that
the differential that was of greatest importance in
affecting people's treatment and view of themselves was
the length of stay in the kibbutz.[21] *Stratification* was
pronounced despite the equality in the distribution of
income.

What stratification and inequality do to people—
their perceptions of themselves, their sense of satisfaction, their feeling of acceptance—are important: the
demand for "Black Power" is as much about the psy-
chology of equality as about the politics of participation.

NOTES

1. We do not discuss mass and other styles of culture. But
   issues of culture will probably reemerge as important;
   they have done so very forcefully in regard to black
   culture and history.
2. Robert W. Hodge, Paul M. Siegel, and Peter H. Rossi,
   "Occupational Prestige in the United States: 1925–
   1963," in Reinhard Bendix and S. M. Lipset, eds., *Class
   Status and Power* (New York: The Free Press, 1966),
   p. 325, table 1.

3. Studies of communities have revealed the stratification and exclusion which occur. Cf. Robert S. Lynd and Helen M. Lynd, *Middletown: A Study in Contemporary American Culture* (New York: Harcourt, Brace and Company, 1929); W. Lloyd Warner, *American Life: Dream and Reality* (Chicago: The University of Chicago Press, 1953); Arthur Vidich and Joseph Bensman, *Small Town in Mass Society* (Princeton: Princeton University Press, 1958); E. S. Bogardus, "Measuring Social Distance," *Journal of Applied Sociology*, IX (1925), 299–308.

4. Former Assistant Secretary of the Treasury Stanley S. Surrey has suggested that tax savings that accrue to individuals and groups from preferences or loopholes in the tax law should be reported as federal "expenditures." If this were done, the Commerce Department would show $1 billion for aiding business in the form of special deductions. *The New York Times,* November 12, 1967. Fifty-five per cent of total 1963 government payments to farmers went to the top 11 per cent of all farmers, those with farm sales of $20,000 and over. Theodore Schultz, "Public Approaches to Minimize Poverty," in Leo Fishman, ed., *Poverty Amid Affluence* (New Haven: Yale University Press, 1966). Cf. Philip M. Stern, *The Great Treasury Raid* (New York: Random House, Inc., 1964).

5. Schultz, *op. cit.* In 1968 the system of government regulation and subsidization of farm crops cost taxpayers more than $5 billion, and over 16,000 persons received more than $25,000 for a total of $5.8 million. *The New York Times,* June 1, 1969, Editorial Section, p. 6.

6. Joseph Goldman, "Progress Report: Welfare Declaration

175

Project," Center for Social Research, The City University of New York, submitted to the New York City Department of Welfare (June 30, 1967).

7. Welfare Declaration Research Project (Joseph Goldman, director), "Use of 'Declaration' in Determining Eligibility for Public Assistance: The City of New York Department of Social Service," Center for Social Research, The City University of New York, HEW Project No. 260, Progress Report III (August 7, 1968).

8. Jonathan Spivak, "Replacing Welfare: A New Way to Help the Poor," *The Wall Street Journal,* October 11, 1968. Another proposal, the children's allowance, may be tested in Gary, Ind., through the Model Cities program. For a discussion of the children's allowance, see James C. Vadakin, *Children, Poverty, and Family Allowances* (New York: Basic Books, Inc., 1968). For guaranteed annual income proposals, see Christopher Green, *Negative Taxes and the Poverty Problem* (Washington, D.C.: The Brookings Institute, 1967); James Tobin, "On Improving the Economic Status of the Negro," *Daedalus,* XCIV, No. 4 (Fall 1965); J. G. Speth, Jr., Richard Cotton, J. C. Bell, H. V. Mindus, "A Model Negative Income Tax Statute," *The Yale Law Journal,* LXXVIII, No. 2 (December 1968); Robert Theobald, *Free Men and Free Markets* (New York: Clarkson N. Potter, 1963); and Robert Theobald, ed., *The Guaranteed Income: Next Step in Economic Evolution?* (Garden City, N.Y.: Doubleday and Company, 1966).

9. As elsewhere in this book, we assume that we are dealing with a group defined economically in class terms, and that we are pursuing the political and social behavior components of this class group. Frequently, there

is little convergence among the groups defined in class, political, or social terms.

10. The link between styles of life and their interpretation is not perfect because, as Lockwood has pointed out with regard to affluent manual employees whom he terms the "new working class," to display the life styles of those "above" and to be accepted by those "above" are two quite different things. David Lockwood, "The New Working Class," *European Journal of Sociology,* I, No. 2 (1960).

11. Other strata are also likely to be viewed as heterogeneous groupings. Cf. S. M. Miller, "The American Lower Class: A Typological Approach," *Social Research* (Spring 1964); and Harold Wilensky, "Mass Society and Mass Culture," in Bernard Berelson and Morris Janowitz, eds., *Reader in Public Opinion and Communication* (New York: The Free Press, 1966).

12. S. M. Miller and Frank Riessman, *Social Class and Social Policy* (New York: Basic Books, Inc., 1968).

13. Harold Wilensky, "Varieties of Work Experience," in Henry Borow, ed., *Man in a World of Work* (Boston: Houghton Mifflin Company, 1964), p. 137.

14. Norman M. Bradburn and David Caplovitz, *Reports on Happiness: A Pilot Study of Behavior Related to Mental Health* (Chicago: Aldine Publishing Company, 1965). Cf. Susan R. Orden and Norman M. Bradburn, "Dimensions of Marriage Happiness," *The American Journal of Sociology,* LXXIII, No. 6 (May 1968). N. M. Bradburn, *The Structure of Psychological Well-Being* (Chicago: Aldine Press, 1969).

15. August B. Hollingshead and Frederic Redlich, *Social*

Class and Mental Illness (New York: John Wiley & Sons, 1958), p. 232.

16. Srole and his associates surveyed midtown Manhattan by interviewing a cross section of residents in their homes. Persons classified as *well* rose steadily from 9.7 per cent in the lowest socioeconomic category (F) to 24.4 per cent in the highest (A): those classified as *impaired* declined from 33.7 per cent to 16.4 per cent in the second highest category and then rose slightly to 17.5 per cent in the highest SES. The term *incapacitated* was applied to category F, 3.3 per cent of category B, and 1.9 per cent of category A. Studies of this kind are subject to the criticism that similar symptoms may not have the same implications and intensity in groups differentially placed in society. L. Srole, T. S. Langner, S. T. Michael, M. K. Opler, and T. A. C. Rennie, *Mental Health in the Metropolis* (New York: McGraw-Hill Book Company, 1962).

17. Cf. Bradburn and Caplovitz, *op. cit.*; G. Gurin, J. Veroff, and S. Feld, *Americans View Their Mental Health* (New York: Basic Books, Inc., 1960); Srole, Langner, Michael, Opler, and Rennie, *op cit.*; Derek L. Phillips, "Social Participation and Happiness," *American Journal of Sociology*, LXXII, No. 5 (March 1967).

18. Bradburn and Caplovitz, *op. cit.*, p. 11.

19. *Ibid.*, pp. 46, 63.

20. W. G. Runciman, *Relative Deprivation and Social Justice: A Study of Attitudes to Social Inequality in Twentieth Century England* (Berkeley: University of California Press, 1966). Also see Robert McKenzie and Allan Silver, *Angels in Marble: Working Class Con-*

servatives in Urban England (Chicago: University of Chicago Press, 1968).

21. Eva Rosenfeld, "Social Stratification in a Classless Society," *American Social Review*, XVI (December 1951).

9
Toward a Redefinition of Well-Being

Casting the concept of poverty in terms of stratification leads to regarding poverty as an issue of inequality. With this approach, we have moved away from efforts to measure poverty lines with pseudoscientific accuracy. Instead, we examined the nature and size of the differences that exist between the bottom 20 or 10 per cent or perhaps the bottom 50 per cent and the rest of society. Our concern becomes one of narrowing the differences in each stratification dimension between those at the bottom and the better-off.

In reshaping many of the issues of poverty into stratificational questions, we do not imply that the poor are a fixed, homogeneous group, sharing a common outlook. Rather, we see the poor as those who lag behind the rest of society in terms of one or more dimensions of life. Considerable turnover occurs in these bottom

180

groups. Although we lack data showing what proportion of persons in the bottom groups move in and out of poverty, we do know that a life-cycle rather than inter-generational pattern is of some importance: the risk of being at the bottom is much greater for older individuals.[1] "Getting old" as well as "beginning poor" increases the chances of poverty. There is undoubtedly greater turnover in the bottom 20 per cent of the population than is commonly believed by those who stress the inheritance and culture of poverty. Even with a high turnover, however, moral and policy questions about the "acceptable" size and kinds of disparities among Americans remain important.

We hope that our effort to place poverty action issues in the context of social stratification is not merely a translation from one language of discourse to another. Therefore, we ask what would be done differently if poverty problems were seen as issues of stratification.

First, we believe that poverty programs would aim for higher targets. Reforming the social structure so that the differences among individuals are reduced usually requires higher goals than bringing individuals up to a rather low economic standard.

Second, a stratificational approach requires constant adjustment of the targets because, as the higher-income groups advance, new levels and kinds of concerns for the lower-income groups emerge. A fixed level of well-being—"a minimum survival standard"—is no longer the aim.

Third, a stratificational approach implies that economic goals are not the only important objectives. Frequently, the economic goal of raising incomes to a $3,000 level has been treated as though it were the only significant target. The multidimensional concerns of stratification force attention to the noneconomic aspects of inequality.

Fourth, we see that changes and shifts in one dimension do not automatically produce changes in other dimensions. Economic gain does not insure automatic attainment of other goals. Indeed, much of contemporary stratificational analysis concerns this problem, and much of the difficulty with appraisal of poverty strategies is that little is known about the multiplier effect of each strategy.[2]

Fifth, a stratificational approach suggests that style-of-life variables may be important in the construction and conduct of poverty programs. This statement does not suggest a "culture of poverty" but an effort to make policies and programs relevant and appropriate to the life styles of their intended consumers.

Sixth, we see that many programs aimed at moving youths out of poverty have neglected vital dimensions of their lives. Many social mobility programs have aimed at enhancing the prospects of youths without improving the conditions of their families. Other programs have sought to improve the education of children without improving the schools which they attend. Head Start and Job Corps, for example, have attempted to create a parallel educational system rather than change the basic educational institutions. In these

182

instances, the social setting of behavior has been neglected.

Seventh, poverty discussions tend to focus narrowly either on the "doors" approach of social mobility through education or the "floors" approach of income maintenance and jobs. A stratificational perspective embraces both approaches—individual change within existing structures and the necessity of change of the structure if those left behind are not to be stigmatized.

Conventional poverty discussions are superficial because they are cast in terms of nineteenth-century concerns about pauperism and subsistence rather than in twentieth-century terms of redistribution. Congress is not clear about the goals of poverty reduction and inequality reduction because the polity has not forthrightly discussed fundamental objectives.

Social scientists bear a heavy fault here. When poverty is viewed in the stratificational perspective, it becomes clear that the goal of bringing all families up to a certain income level cloaks disagreements about the relative importance of differing, often conflicting, objectives. For example, in the objectives of efforts to change the stratificational system, is the goal a classless society with only minor differences among individuals? Or is the goal a meritocracy in which individuals have in actuality equal access to high-level jobs which are highly rewarded? Or is the target to connect an underclass, which does not improve its conditions as much as the rest of the society, into the processes which will begin to make it less distinctive? Or do we seek to reduce the gaps in some vital dimensions between the nonpoor and the poor? Each of these views implies a belief concerning what is important about stratificational systems, how permeable these systems are, and how other goals should be balanced against the concern with the underclasses.

In emphasizing the importance of inequality and its varied forms, we are not implicitly arguing the case for complete equality—that there should be no distinctions among individuals. Rather, we believe that many inequalities are much greater than most realize and that they are hard to defend even on the basis of a narrow, economically rational allocation of benefits. We are also critical of them on the basis of our own view of what constitutes a desirable society.[3]

It could be argued that unconscious inequality is preferable to conscious inequality; that is, if society is unaware of the degree of inequality and the processes leading to it, less is demanded of the disadvantaged individuals than when consciously selected processes sort out the disadvantaged. This danger is eloquently expressed by Michael Young in *The Rise of the Meritocracy*. However, we do find it hard to accept the notion that *at this time* unawareness of inequalities is more kind to the disadvantaged than public discussion of these inequalities. Perry Anderson has stated this need well:

Considered only in terms of opportunity and power, class [that is, inequality] appears as a unilateral possession of privileges, a greater accumulation of benefits and powers in one sector of society than another. But class is clearly more than this. It is a universal loss. There is one human need it violates in all members of society, oppressors and oppressed alike; the need of men for each other. It is in its aspects as a pure human *division*, rather than an economic or political disparity, which is most often ignored and yet which wholly describe class.[4]

One does not need to embrace the idea of complete equality to feel that reductions in inequality are desirable.[5]

The fact that many of the poor in the United States would be well off in low-income societies suggests that more is involved in poverty than just low-levels in the physical conditions of life. The issues of relative deprivation appear to be more important. In that perspective, we must increasingly turn to the indicators of inequality as well as to poverty, which implies a scientific standard of subsistence. The last third of the twentieth century requires new and more sensitive instruments than existed in the nineteenth century.

Poverty is *income-insufficiency*, but in the affluent society it is more than that. To be able to discuss poverty and inequality requires an understanding of the changing dynamic and desirable products of the society. As in many other cases the situation of the poor is forcing social scientists and actionists to understand better the society in which the disturbing questions of humanity still haunt the economic cornucopia. For example, the indictment of education because of its inadequate development of low-income youths has probably improved education for all. *The issues of distribution—who should get what—inevitably lead to questioning the character of the "what."* Part II discusses this question.

The stratification perspective that has been developed in Part I has led us to see that in dealing with poverty we are dealing with the *quality of life* of individuals, and not just their economic positions. This means that not only individuals' relationships to government but the *quality of relationships among people* in society are important. Although governmental and organizational action is needed to diminish the economic and political inequalities that separate people, we as individuals must assume responsibility for changing the quality of relationships among ourselves and others. Ultimately, change in the distribution of social honor and self-respect, the most fundamental aspects of stratification, can only be accomplished by each of us, members of society, caring about the excluded and breaking down the walls of social and psychological exclusion. If poverty is about stratification, we cannot escape one another.

NOTES

1. Since the aged have different needs and consumption patterns than younger persons, it may make more sense to think in terms of stratification within the aged. Inci-

186

dentally, there is a greater concentration of income among those above sixty-five than among any other age group.

2. See Martin Rein and S. M. Miller, "Poverty, Policy, and Purpose: The Dilemmas of Choice," in Leonard H. Goodman, ed., *Economic Progress and Social Welfare* (New York: Columbia University Press, 1966).

3. For interesting discussions of inequality, see W. G. Runciman, *Relative Deprivation and Social Justice* (Berkeley: University of California Press, 1966); Bertram de Jouvenal, *The Ethics of Redistribution* (New York: Cambridge University Press, 1952); Lee Rainwater, "Towards a Society of Average Men," unpublished; Robin Blackburn, "Inequality and Exploitation," *New Left Review*, No. 42 (March–April 1967).

4. Perry Anderson, "Sweden: A Study in Social Democracy," *New Left Review*, No. 9 (May 1961).

5. See S. M. Miller and Martin Rein, "Poverty, Inequality and Policy," in Howard S. Becker, ed., *Social Problems* (New York: John Wiley & Sons, 1966).

PART II

Social Policies of the Future

10
From Inequality
to Social Change

When we began this book, we hoped to move from the explication of the facts of inequality in Part I to a projection of the likely contours and extent of inequality in the 1970's and later. The book could not be contained within these systematic limits. As we explored the future of inequality, we were led into examination of the basic issue of what was going to be produced and of how well this output would meet "need." While economic inequality will be important, the issues of the relations between the individual and government and among individuals will grow in importance for all Americans, not only for the less equal.

We rediscovered the fact with which we started: to discuss inequality requires attention to all in society, not only to those left behind in economic expansion of the economy.

In short, we have been forced to examine the future as an American problem rather than as the problem of the less equal.

Not only gloom but hope produces the issues of the future. The inconsistencies that exist between our possibilities and our realities as well as the pain of our realities create social problems. As the feasible expands, new aims and expectations emerge. As old goals are reached or made obsolete, new goals evolve, which demand new solutions. These new demands will represent new problems. Thus, it is not only *structural strains,* the conflicts among institutionalized behaviors, which cause social problems, but the distance between our stars and our earth, our hopes and anticipations and the slow-moving present.

It is not only the failure of institutions, producing gloom and a sense of doom, which causes unrest, but the failure to realize new possibilities or new hopes. Increasingly, these new expectations center on the quality of human relations. By what means will the nation obtain a higher quality of living and by what standards will it be measured? How should its goods be shared? What will be the form, functions, and purposes of government? What balance will be established between individual freedom and social stability? Toward what ends will the materially affluent society strive?

We believe that these questions will be the foremost

issues of the future; indeed they have been basic problems in all societies, both past and present.[1] They appear to be universal questions in all but utopian states. We learn how to deal badly or well with these issues; we do not learn to escape them.

Continuity or change may loom large when one views the future. To see the future only in terms of continuity is to be guilty of presentism, that is, to emphasize current issues as though they have lasting and deep import. To stress change seems to lead contemporary writers into a compulsive attraction to the projection of technological trends, leading to the neglect of social issues. We believe that despite the technological possibilities of the 1970's, the problems of the 1960's, which centered on poverty and race, will not rapidly disappear but will continue as main elements of the nation's moral agenda. Nor will the vision of a post-industrial society safeguard us from the clash of interests and purposes.

In the following chapters projections calculated by federal and private agencies help us to form an image of how these abstract issues will appear in the next ten to thirty years. The mid-to-late 1970's will primarily concern us.

In order to limit the scope of our discussion, we shall concentrate on a narrow span of domestic problems. We shall not discuss the critical issues of war and peace, the development of low-income societies, or the establishment of a stronger world government. We shall ignore the fact that the issues of the world condition

American life. We shall focus on amenities, the issues involved in the provision of a modern living; inequality, the distribution of societal goods and services; the participation in and the effectiveness of governments; the balance between individual autonomy and social stability; and authenticity in the efficient, affluent society.

NOTE

1. For a summary of other approaches to the study of the future, see Henry Winthrop, "The Sociologist and the Study of the Future," *The American Sociologist*, III, No. 2 (May 1968), 136–145. The major recent works on the future include "Toward the Year 2000," *Daedalus*, XCVI, No. 3 (Summer 1967); Herman Kahn and Anthony J. Wiener, *The Year 2000: A Framework for Speculation on the Next Thirty-three Years* (New York: The Macmillan Company, 1967); Daniel Bell, "The Study of the Future," *The Public Interest* (Fall 1965), pp. 119–130; Donald N. Michael, *The Next Generation: The Prospects Ahead for the Use of Today and Tomorrow* (New York: Random House, Inc., 1965); Kenneth Boulding, *The Meaning of the Twentieth Century* (New York: Harper and Row, 1964).

194

11
Amenities: Providing a Decent, Modern Level of Living for All

In 1880, the population of the United States was about 50 million; in forty years, it doubled to 105 million in 1920. In the 50 years since 1920, it increased by 100 million and passed the 200 million mark. Thus, the absolute number that is being added to the population is much greater than it was in earlier years. For example, not quite 19 million people were added to the population between 1950 and 1960; between 1967 and 1977, the increase is expected to be 35 million persons.[1] How will such large and rapid increases during the next decades affect the attainment of a decent level of living for all?

195

Delivering the services and amenities that are presently taken for granted in the United States to 35 million additional people will absorb a sizable portion of the expected increase in the gross national product (GNP). The task of providing an adequate standard of living for all is even more difficult because, in addition to the task of continuing to deliver the *present* standards of living to a growing population, the nation has already set *new* goals for itself. In 1960, one such set of goals was identified by President Eisenhower's Commission on National Goals (see Table 11–1). In 1975, the nation will still be attempting to achieve these goals. The rate at which the nation realizes these new standards of living will be limited by the continued population growth and by the difficulties of expanding the nation's economic growth rate beyond certain limits without risking "unacceptable" price increases, upsetting the United States' balance of gold payments, or imposing serious governmental restrictions upon economic behavior (for example, price and wage controls).

In 1966 the National Planning Association estimated that realizing the goals that were set in 1960 plus the new space goals will cost the nation $1.1 trillion in the year 1975. This figure exceeds the estimated GNP for 1975 by $150 billion (15 per cent of the GNP expected in that year).[2]

Not only limited economic resources but also limited manpower will restrict the rate at which the nation will be able to achieve its goals. In 1968 Lecht estimated that full achievement of the sixteen national

196

TABLE 11-1 Gross Expenditures for Individual Goals: 1962 and 1975 (in millions of 1962 dollars)

Goal	Actual Expenditures, 1962	Projected Expenditures, 1975 for Preempted Benchmarks[a]	Projected Expenditures, 1975 for Aspiration Standards	Per Cent Increase in Expenditures, 1962 to 1975, Aspiration Standards
Consumer expenditures and savings	$356,750	$472,600	$ 659,600	85
Private plant and equipment	48,900	102,300	151,600	209
Urban development	64,200	83,300	129,700	102
Social welfare	38,250	55,450	92,400	142
Health	32,300	39,100	85,400	164
Education	29,700	39,700	82,100	176
Transportation	35,150	56,150	74,900	113
National defense	51,450	39,050	67,550	32
Housing	29,400	36,300	62,000	111
Research and development	16,850	29,700	38,850	131
Natural resources	5,850	7,100	16,650	183
International aid	5,400	3,100	12,250	126
Space	3,300	5,700	9,350	181
Agriculture	7,200	5,200	9,150	26[b]
Manpower retraining	100	400	2,850	
Area redevelopment	350	450	950	186
Total gross cost	$725,150	$975,600	$1,495,300	
−Double accounting	190,000	206,000	368,000	
Estimated net cost	$535,000	$769,600	$1,127,300	
Gross national product	$556,000		$ 981,000	

[a]The increases in spending beyond the 1962 levels of cost for the preempted benchmarks are primarily due to population increase, and they assume no improvement in the quality of our society's performance. The larger expenditures for the aspiration standards include the additional costs of expanding our objectives in each of the areas. The aspiration standards for the sixteen goals are discussed in detail in Lecht, loc. cit. The aspiration standards are based upon what experts in each of the fields regard as desirable achievement, given that the specific goals under consideration were to have high priority. Because other estimates of the total cost of achieving all sixteen national goals have not been made, we are unable to assess this estimate as either liberal or conservative.

[b]Since the federal retraining programs were just getting underway in 1962, a percentage increase computed from 1962 as the base would be misleading.

SOURCE: Leonard A. Lecht, Goals, Priorities, and Dollars: The Next Decade (New York: The Free Press, 1966), pp. 36, 40.

goals by the mid-1970's would require an employed civilian labor force of more than a 100 million, about 10 million more than are expected to be in the civilian labor force by 1975.[3]

Given these limited economic and manpower resources, a number of variables in addition to population growth will affect the extent to which American society will achieve these articulated social goals. The larger the nation's defense budget becomes, the more limited will be the share of resources for nondefense goals. The geographic distribution of the urban population will affect the cost and therefore the realization of social welfare, health, and educational standards. Reduced suburban population densities will increase the costs of achieving these social standards. Advances in educational attainment and general knowledge may enable the nation's population to obtain greater benefits from the country's limited resources. Hopefully, technological developments and new products will also lead to more effective utilization of the nation's limited resources.

On the other hand, byproducts of technology, such as air pollution, will present exceedingly costly problems. Achieving a high standard of living may require not only moving to new standards but also reacquiring old standards of clean air and water.

Not only is it unlikely that goals established in 1960 will be met by 1975, but by then the nation's goals will have been expanded by a generation of new expectations if the consumer spurt continues. For these reasons, achieving what will be considered an adequate standard of living for all is likely to be a major material and physical difficulty during the mid-1970's.[4]

In the following discussion we will examine more concretely the issues and problems involved in meeting our social goals in health, education, and welfare and the goals for our cities in housing, transportation, and urban development.[5]

HEALTH, EDUCATION, AND WELFARE

A shortage of adequately trained manpower will be the primary problem confronting the nation in health, education, and welfare. A large increase in the number of persons performing teaching, medical, and other service roles will be required for professional services to merely keep pace with the population increase. The nation's chances of meeting these manpower needs rest primarily upon its ability to pull in and effectively use minority persons since they are the greatest source of unutilized talent.

It is certain that manpower needs will not be met because the cost of training an increasing proportion of the nation's population to fill professional and social welfare requirements competes with other uses for economic resources. The health field sharply mirrors these issues. Despite the enormous funds that are spent on health measures, the United States currently lags behind other countries in maintaining the health of its people. Both its infant mortality rates and its mortality rates for working-age males are higher than those in many Western European nations.[6]

Between 1965 and 1975, the number of medical schools is expected to increase from 86 to 126.[7] Despite this increase, the nation will be faced with the problem of a growing shortage of doctors; the nation's demand for physicians will increase by approximately 34 per cent, while the number of physicians will increase by approximately 17 per cent. Despite the need for doctors, fully qualified applicants will continue to be turned away from medical schools unless current policies are radically and unexpectedly changed.

Education is also likely to suffer from severe manpower shortages. The United States' school-age population (ages five to twenty-four) is expected to grow from 70.2 million in early 1967 to more than 105 million in 1975, and to 125 million by the year 2000.[8] College enrollments are expected to expand even more rapidly than elementary and high school enrollments. Undergraduate college students are expected to number 15 to 20 million by the year 2000, as compared with 5.5 million in 1967. The body of graduate students is expected to quadruple from 0.5 million in 1967 to between 2 and 2.5 million by the end of the century.[9] Thus, not only the increase in our school-age population, but the longer, perhaps lifelong, education seemingly required by technological needs will increase rapidly the need for teachers and educational facilities.

Education, increasingly the dominant route to social

mobility, will continue to be a relatively scarce resource, subject to bitter political wrangling about its cost control and efficiency as well as its distribution. The acrimonious demand for open enrollment of disadvantaged students—despite their low high school grades and the constricted budgets of colleges—illustrate the push towards college education and the constraints of finances.

Maintaining the existing modes of education and training and the prevailing entrance requirements for jobs will insure that an inadequate number of persons will be available for higher-level jobs. Credentialism, unless curtailed, will produce labor shortages as individuals who could perform well are not given the opportunity to obtain good jobs or to get promoted into them. In the 1970's the need is not only for better training and education but also for developing those individuals who cannot cope with the present formal educational system and for providing new routes into and up the job scale.

HOUSING, TRANSPORTATION, AND URBAN DEVELOPMENT

The issues involved in developing adequate standards of urban living must be seen in broader terms than manpower. They will involve technical as well as economic, political, and social problems.

Providing a sufficient supply of decent housing is probably the major technological-economic failure of industrial societies. Even in Sweden, considered to be the model welfare state, new families must expect a

long wait for housing. In the United States, each year
more housing becomes aged and outdated in its style;
a fraction of this aged housing, which is also in poor
physical condition, is torn down. During the next decades, not only the condition but the sheer availability
of housing will be a central problem in metropolitan
areas because of the rapidly rising urban population.

Issues of housing will be complicated by the location
of new housing. Between 1975 and 1985 the baby-boom
population will be buying housing in the suburbs. By
the year 2000, the majority of the nation will probably
be living in suburban areas.[10] Unless current zoning
regulations are amended, the new single-family homes
will be built on larger and larger lots. Such low-density
suburban living will increase the costs and lower the
possibility of obtaining adequate standards of living
for the entire population. It will further separate
suburbanites from downtown services and cultural centers as well as deface the natural countryside. The costs
of communications, sanitation, transportation, water,
gas, electricity, and education will be increased by
low-density living. Longer power and gas lines will be
required in these developments. Many additional miles
of travel for garbage collection and mail delivery will
be necessary if traditional means are to be employed.

Because of the increased costs of neighborhood
amenities, new suburban governments will attempt to
attract more light industry and to channel more urban
resources and money into suburban rather than central-
city coffers. New low-density areas also mean an in-

creased reliance upon cars because subway systems and other forms of public transportation are feasible only in high-density areas. Even car pools are impractical for individuals who live in low-density suburban areas. The increased reliance upon cars means that more space must be devoted to highways, and that the highways, in turn, will push suburbia further into the space which was once the countryside.[11]

Meanwhile, the needs of center cities will grow. Unskilled rural immigrants will continue to move into the center cities' dingy, crowded blocks. Despite the great emigration from the South between 1950 and 1960, the absolute number of southern blacks has slightly increased, due to high birth rates.[12] Through at least the mid-1970's, poor economic conditions or the lack of public welfare, health, and other basic services will continue to push rural persons as well as immigrants from outside United States boundaries into both southern and northern megalopolitan slums.[13] In 1975, 85 per cent of the United States' black population will be living in cities, as compared with 73 per cent in the early 1960's.[14] The costs of meeting their needs will compete with the costs of developing highways, neighborhood amenities, and social, health, and educational services in sprawling suburbia. The competition between suburbia and the center city is therefore likely to become an increasingly divisive political question.

Not only the provision of adequate housing and transportation, but the troublesome byproducts of technical advances will be costly urban problems. Air pollution

203

resulting from the rapid development of industry and automobiles may be the largest urban problem in search of a relatively inexpensive technological remedy. Harvey S. Perloff when director of Regional and Urban Studies for Resources of the Future warned that, "Unless some startling and currently unforeseen technological advances come along, it may well be that by the turn of the century pure air, far from being free, could require a greater public and private annual outlay than any other single resource."[15] A conservative estimate suggests that $10 billion a year will be required over the next thirty years in order for this nation to obtain manageable levels of air and water pollution.[16] The current discussions about protecting the environment are none too soon and should generate needed and expensive public policies.

IMPLICATIONS

What are the implications of these difficulties which we foresee in attaining a high standard of living in the 1970's? It is unlikely that there will be deterioration below present conditions, or even that we will fail to make substantial gains over the present in most fields. Rather, the easy confidence of affluence, of moving rapidly and effortlessly upward, will be challenged.

Difficult issues of choice will continue to emerge. An important concern will be the division of monies and responsibilities between the public and the private sectors of the economy. What percentage of personal income will be used for things which are collectively consumed? How much will the public allow itself to be taxed?

Within the public sector of expenditures, the issues will center on the division of funds. How much is to be allocated to military and civilian activities. And within civilian spending to education, health, urban activities, policing functions, and the like? The failure of social science to be able to provide firm data and analyses for making these decisions will become more apparent. As costs and taxes rise, the effectiveness of expenditures, especially in the social services, will be increasingly questioned. The existing professional domains, for example, social work, physicians' services, and education, will be criticized for their inability to prove a high degree of effectiveness.

Deeper, more divisive questions lie beneath these issues. The discomforting lesson of the 1960's is that affluence does not produce contentment, nor, for long, complacency. The hopes of the Eisenhower 1950's—that affluence would erode conflict—and of the Johnson 1960's—that consensus would be constructed through the artful balancing of interests—were shattered by the sounds of falling glass in riot-torn areas and the anger of uncomplacent students. The Marxist concern with economic crisis and psychological estrangement leading to conflict was not rejected but drastically changed by affluence, while the Weberian issues of disenchantment and bureaucratic power became political as well as

205

sociopsychological issues. Conflict, strain, and discontent are likely to continue in the 1970's.

The desires to attain a modern standard of living for most Americans and to continually increase that standard will not easily be met. We will go materially onward and upward, but with bubbling dissensions. The increasingly technical aspects of our economic problems do not make them less political or less ideological; they make them more complicated. Solutions are less likely to please many of the diverse interests involved; consequently, dissension and antagonism may grow with the expanded role of the technician and the continued swelling of our national output.

Affluence has given rise to new expectations that will be difficult to reach, and that, even if reached, will not eliminate conflict. Nowhere is this more clear than in the question of the distribution of the benefits of society, to which we now turn.

NOTES

1. The United States population is expected to reach 263 million by 1985 and 340 million by the year 2000 as compared with 200 million in 1967. The population will continue to rise after 1975 even if birth rates decrease, because the "baby-boom" children will have reached reproductive age. Ben Wattenberg and Richard M. Scammon, *This U.S.A.* (Garden City, N.Y.: Doubleday & Company, 1965), p. 299.
2. Leonard A. Lecht, *Goals, Priorities, and Dollars: The*

Next Decade (New York: The Free Press, 1966), p. 19. The National Planning Association's estimate that the 1975 GNP will be $981 billion is based on the assumption that the yearly rate of increase in GNP will be 4.5 per cent. These figures are in real terms discounting price increases. A rate of increase much larger than 4.5 per cent, according to Lecht, would be likely to upset the United States' balance of payments or conflict with other national goals. The NPA's cost estimates do not account for the sources of the funds; the monies could be channeled through either the public or the private sector.

3. Leonard A. Lecht, *Manpower Requirements for National Objectives in the 1970's* (Washington, D.C.: U.S. Department of Labor, Manpower Administration, 1968), p. 39.

4. We assume in this chapter that new goals are purely material and economic. Later, we discuss other non-material goals, such as authenticity.

5. In the following paragraphs, we will not discuss food, clothing, amusements, and other personal items which are included under consumer expenditures in the budget for national goods. See Woodrow Ginsburg and Jerry Anderson, "How Much Will It Take?" *Social Service Outlook*, III, No. 5 (May 1968), for a discussion of these items.

6. National Commission on Technology, Automation, and Economic Progress, *Technology and the American Economy*, I (February 1966), 7. Of course, not all of this difference can be attributed to medical care rather than to other conditions which affect infant mortality like the nutrition of the pregnant mother.

7. Wilbur Cohen, *Social Policies for the Nineteen Seven-*

ties (Washington, D.C.: U.S. Department of Health, Education and Welfare, 1966).

8. U.S. Bureau of the Census, *Current Population Reports,* Population Estimates, Ser. P-25, No. 359 (February 20, 1967).

9. Richard Martin, "Education: The Lifelong School," in The Wall Street Journal Staff, *Here Comes Tomorrow: Living and Working in the Year 2000* (Princeton, N.J.: Dow Jones Books, 1967), p. 163.

10. Wattenberg and Scammon, *op. cit.,* p. 300.

11. See Victor Gruen, "Introduction" in Robert A. Futterman, *The Future of Our Cities* (Garden City, N.Y.: Doubleday & Company, 1961), pp. 6–7.

12. Wattenberg and Scammon, *op. cit.,* p. 300.

13. Will Lissner, "Migration of Poor to City Likely for Decade More," *The New York Times,* August 14, 1967, p. 1; and Bayard Rustin, New York City Planning Commission, *Future by Design,* Symposium (October 1964).

14. Lecht, *op. cit.*

15. Harvey S. Perloff, *The Wall Street Journal,* December 6, 1966.

16. *U.S. News and World Report,* April 3, 1967, pp. 42–45. It is impossible to free the air and water of all pollutants. This estimate is for spending to the point where the dollar costs and benefits of pollution reduction would be roughly equal. Currently air and water pollution does billions of dollars of destruction. One aesthetic example of this destruction is the obelisk in New York City's Central Park which has undergone greater deterioration in thirty years in the city than in over 2,000 years in Egypt. Also see "A Guide for Smog Bound Investors," *Business Week,* July 22, 1967.

12
Inequality:
The Distribution
of Amenities

In the 1920's inequality of income grew; in the 1940's it narrowed; and in the 1960's it remained stable.[1] During the 1970's, inequalities will increase unless there is deliberate manipulation of the economy aimed at reducing them.

The issues of inequality will always be with us because the various groups and sectors of society do not move at the same pace or in the same way. Therefore, in discussing the reduction of inequalities, we do not assume that the goal is complete and final equality. Instead, we are concerned with the rate of reduction or expansion of inequalities.

In this chapter, we shall discuss first the economic and social factors, (including educational changes) that will produce greater inequalities in the 1970's; second, we shall discuss the factors that may promote or hinder the development of conscious policies to reduce inequalities; and third, we shall discuss the consequences of growing inequalities.

FACTORS PRODUCING INEQUALITIES

Economic and social changes will produce greater inequalities in the 1970's. As technology continues to advance and employers increase educational requirements, those at the bottom of society will find that rising to higher positions is increasingly difficult. Groups that are now relatively secure will also become increasingly subject to job instability and its many hardships. These changes are likely to overbalance the inequality-reducing changes initiated by public policy. We shall now look at these structural changes more closely.

OCCUPATIONAL CHANGE

During the 1970's, the distribution of occupations will continue to change rapidly. Between 1949 and 1965, 6,000 new occupational titles appeared in the United States Employment Service's *Dictionary of Occupational Titles*, and 8,000 were dropped from the listing.[2] Although not all the jobs represented by the 8,000 titles that were dropped from the *Dictionary* completely disappeared, these numbers do provide some

210

idea of the magnitude of change occurring within the occupational structure. Where is this change occurring? What segments of the population will it primarily affect?

Table 12–1 compares the projected 1975 occupational distribution of United States labor with the 1967 distribution and shows the educational and racial characteristics of the labor force currently employed within each category.[3] While white-collar jobs are expected to increase by 17 per cent between 1968 and 1975, blue-collar jobs will increase by only 10 per cent. Within the overall occupational distribution, this means that the relative importance of white-collar jobs will increase by 1.2 per cent, while that of blue-collar jobs will decrease by 2.2 per cent. The greatest spurt (21 per cent) in a single occupational category will occur among professional, technical, and kindred workers.

Occupations employing the majority of the black and unskilled labor force will have the smallest growth; 59 per cent of the nonwhite male labor force was employed in blue-collar work (excluding service work) in 1967, and in 1963, 63 per cent of employed non-high school graduates were blue-collar workers.[4] Of the occupations whose employees' median level of educational attainment is under twelve years, only service jobs are expected to increase proportionately in the overall occupational distribution. Thus, the plight of blacks, Mexican-Americans, and Puerto Ricans will be, in large part, the plight of the low-educated.

Not only the decreasing availability of unskilled work

TABLE 12-1 Employment Projections by Major Occupation Group and Employment Characteristics (male and female)

Major Occupation Group	Per Cent Change, 1967-1975	1975[a]	Percentage Distribution March 1967[b]			Median School Years Completed, March 1967	
			Total Both Sexes	White Males	Nonwhite Males	White Male	Nonwhite Male
Total employment (number in millions)		88.7	70.6	40.7	4.4	40.7	4.3
Professional, technical, and kindred workers	+1.0	14.9	13.9	14.4	7.0	16.3	16.2
Manager, officials, and proprietors, except farm	+0.1	10.4	10.3	14.8	3.6	12.8	12.1
Clerical and kindred workers	−0.1	16.5	16.6	7.2	8.3	12.5	12.4
Sales workers	+0.4	6.5	6.1	6.0		12.8	12.4
Craftsmen, foremen, and kindred workers	−0.8	12.8	13.4	21.2	12.9	12.0	10.1
Operatives and kindred workers	−2.2	16.7	18.9	19.7	28.2	11.1	10.0
Laborers, except farm and mine	+0.1	4.2	4.1	4.9	17.7	9.9	8.6
Service workers	+4.0	14.1	10.1	6.2	15.2	11.8	10.3
Farm workers			1.6	1.4	4.5	8.6	5.8

a National Commission on Technology, Automation, and Economic Progress, The Outlook for Technological Change and Employment (Washington D.C.: U.S. Government Printing Office, February 1966), I, 133, Appendix A.

b U.S. Department of Labor, Bureau of Labor Statistics, "Educational Attainment of Workers," Monthly Labor Review (February 1968), p. A-15, table J.

opportunities, but also geographical shifts in jobs will make entry into the occupational structure increasingly difficult for persons lacking higher degrees. In all parts of the nation, labor-force statisticians are pointing to dwindling job opportunities for the poor in center cities. Factories and stores that employ less-educated workers are moving to the suburbs. A United States Bureau of Labor Statistics study of twelve metropolitan areas found that between 1959 and 1965, payroll employment rose two and a half times as fast in the suburbs as in the total metropolitan areas.[5] The future trend will be much the same. In St. Louis, for example, 10,000 of the 12,000 jobs that are expected to open up in the next five years will be in the suburbs.[6] Unless low-income as well as high-income homes are constructed near these new jobs, workers will be forced to commute long distances to work. Such commuting is particularly difficult for low-income persons. Driving long distances could be a prohibitive cost in a worker's budget; unless great improvements are made, public transportation may consume half again as much time as the working day itself.[7] Therefore, as outlined in Chapter 5, a minimum level of access to modern, efficient, public transportation will be important.

While unskilled factory jobs will be reduced by automatic machines and materials handling equipment or moved from the center to the periphery of cities, the skill requirements of middle-level jobs will rise, making more difficult the advance of the low educated.[8] Routine, repetitive tasks of managers and professionals

213

will be computerized and thus eliminated as human tasks. In the year 2000, the United States farmer, like the automobile manufacturer, will be a sophisticated urban executive with a computer for a foreman. Similarly, much of the routine work of lawyers, medical doctors, librarians, and accountants will be eliminated by computers. As a consequence of these changes, those at the bottom of society will not only be faced with the elimination of unskilled work, but will need to attain greater expertise to qualify for and keep up with skilled and professional positions. Education will be more crucial for all.

EDUCATIONAL CHANGE

The distribution of education and of educational resources is important because education has intrinsic value and provides a means by which individuals obtain other valued ends—material well-being, power, and status. During the next thirty years, the nation's population will obtain an increasing amount of formal education. In 1967, the median educational attainment for persons aged twenty-five to twenty-nine was 12.5 years. By the year 2000, it will probably be 14.0 years, that is, two years of college, or more.[9] High school graduates will comprise an estimated 63 per cent of the total United States population in 1985, as compared with 45 per cent of the population in 1965 and 34 per cent of the population in 1950.[10] Between 1965 and 1985, college enrollments are expected to nearly double, from 5 million to about 9.5 million.[11]

214

The expected statistical increase in formal education will not resolve educational problems. First, increasing individuals' knowledge and skills not only increases the nation's human resources but paradoxically wastes these resources and creates national tensions. By reducing the gateways to occupations to one, that of education, we are barring many capable individuals from jobs they could perform well. For the nation to obtain high levels of employment and efficient use of manpower, jobs need to be broken down into tasks that do and these that do not require many years of formal education.[12]

Second, educational, especially higher educational, resources are unevenly distributed. Therefore, our educational sorting system does *not* work as a perfect meritocracy, as many would like to believe. As noted in Chapter 6, the unevenness of the distribution of education between inner city and suburban areas is increasing.

With the increasing demand for college credentials, the distribution of higher educational resources will be more important. To date, federal as well as state and local governmental funds have been directed primarily toward the nonpoor. Colleges and universities must seriously confront the question of how they are to adapt to the needs of the low-income, inner-city student. This question extends far beyond the relatively simple granting of admission and financial aid. Among other issues, it will involve the geographical location of institutions of higher education. Because vacant land exists far from the inner city and the costs of building near the core are increasing, universities, like factories and stores, are moving to the periphery of our cities. The farther colleges are built from the low-income sector of the city and from mass public transportation, the more they exclude youths whose families cannot afford the extra cars and other transportation to reach them.

More important than getting low-income and minority students into college is getting them through college with a useful experience. This would require not only relocating colleges or providing remedial training so that low-income students can grapple with college courses, but restructuring the college so that all students can benefit from and contribute to learning within it.[13]

Before the year 2000, more *pseudomeritocracies*, rather than full meritocracies, are likely to develop. As Young shows, both have grave problems.[14] Meritocracies and mass education do not increase equality; as Jencks and Riesman point out, they merely make the criteria for mobility more impersonal.[15]

Education once served to free society, at least partially, from the rule of nepotism and arbitrariness. Educational qualifications rivaled "connections." Standards which applied to almost everyone meant that the rewards of privilege were less than before. But today education, the hope of previous generations, has become a barrier to the occupational ascendancy of the poor and the discriminated. The narrowing of routes to economic opportunity is a problem which will grow in importance during the 1970's.

216

FACTORS PROMOTING AND IMPEDING
REDISTRIBUTIVE POLICIES

The trends reviewed in Chapter 2 show that the economy, if left to itself, will not lead to inequality reduction. Only deliberate public policy can lead to greater equality. Will the nation develop public policies sufficient to reduce inequalities, or to even prevent them from growing?

What factors may promote policies to reduce inequalities? Civil rights groups and Poor People's groups may generate renewed political pressure for policies to reduce inequalities during the 1970's. The nation may also support such policies because of its fear of riots and ever-growing national disturbances, rather than because of a positive commitment to the reduction of inequalities. Unfortunately, such fear frequently results in greater pressure for police control rather than in programs for inequality reduction. The 1968 United States Kerner Riot Commission report was an exception. Instead of calling for greater police control, it clearly stated that the nation can counteract the violence ripping American streets only by fighting the widening gap between the human needs of the poor and the nonpoor and by ending the destruction in the lives of many people within our affluent society.[16] Making the good beginning provided by the Commission into something more than just another report will require the political support of the nation.

Successful inequality-reduction policies are possible.

Although we do not want to overstate the progress that was made by federal efforts to reduce inequalities during the 1960's—for these efforts were indeed small when viewed in the perspective of total local, state, and federal expenditures—we feel it is important to point out that some progress *has* been made. Education is the most striking example. Between 1960 and 1966 federal spending on education increased by 310 per cent, from $3.1 to $9.6 billion, and the percentage of these funds going to children of low-income families increased from 10 to 26 per cent.[17] The percentage of federal health expenditures going to the poor also increased during this period. These increases must be treated with caution because we are not certain of how much of the increased spending recorded as "for the poor" actually was used by the poor.[18] Nonetheless, the experience of the mid-1960's appears to show that with increased federal spending, it is possible to allocate much of the marginal increase to the poor.

The single most important inequality-reduction effort is a sustained, high-employment economy which provides a forced draft demand for workers who would not be hired under less pressured economic expansion. The achievement of high rates of economic growth will be one of the great and difficult requirements of the 1970's.

A more progressive tax system, reducing the disproportionate impact of all taxes on the poor and the near-poor, would also make a substantial difference, provided the rich paid a higher share of their income in taxes than they now do in practice.

218

The expansion and improvement of income maintenance procedures would be another way of offsetting
the inequalities produced by the economic marketplace.
The issue is not only the structure of this additional
income to persons—whether family allowance, or negative income tax, or welfare reform—but, more importantly, the level of expenditures necessary to right the
inequalities induced by unregulated markets.

In the 1970's, the nation is obviously more likely to
support programs for inequality reduction if it is not
burdened with heavy defense spending. Indeed, in a
period of peace, corporations are likely to actively seek
domestic programs in which they may invest.

Although these factors give us hope that the nation
will support some inequality-reduction policies, we do
not expect the development of adequate inequality
measures. Many obstacles stand in the way of stronger
inequality-reduction policies. Among the major difficulties will be changing such hard-to-reach but important
dimensions of inequality as the distribution of respect
and obtaining popular support for policies that improve
not only the absolute but the relative position of politically weak groups.

First, inequality is very complicated. Government
policies can have only limited impact on the reduction
of many forms of inequality. Public policy can tear
down legal barriers to social interaction and may even
equalize incomes, services, and amenities, but these
changes only limitedly affect the distribution of respect.
The granting of respect and dignity, basic needs of all
men, cannot be legislated; they must be given by one

man to another. Ultimately, it is the underlying distribution of self-respect and the granting of respect
which make the other issues of inequality important in
societies where no one is starving.

Second, it is unlikely that the growth of the economy
will reduce income inequalities.[19] Therefore, conscious
public policies will be needed. These inequality-reducing policies require a high degree of popular support.
The slow, blundering process of acquiring majority support for any public reform is a problem which accom-
panies the advantages of democratic structures. Gaining support for inequality reduction is especially
difficult because the middle classes, like every political
group, are primarily interested in raising their own
standards of living.

Obtaining popular support is made more difficult by
the recognition that significant change in the correction
of inequality of conditions frequently requires inequality of opportunity. Compensatory employment,
compensatory college selection, such as Harvard's practice of admitting black students on different entrance
criteria than white students, and compensatory educational programs will be required to overcome the
inequalities which have built up over the past.

For any or perhaps all of the dimensions of inequality
to be reduced, funds and manpower must be selectively
channeled to those who are lagging behind. Univer-
salistic policies that are aimed at simultaneously improving the conditions of all in society do not reduce
the distance between those at the top and those at the
bottom.

The reduction of inequalities requires not only absolute but relative gains by those who are lagging behind. If the children of the poor obtain three more years of education than their parents while the children of the well-to-do also gain proportionately in years of education, the children of the poor will not gain bargaining power in the occupational marketplace. If the distance between persons who rank high and low on economic and social ladders is to be reduced, more resources and opportunities must be channeled to those who lag behind than to others in society.

In the 1970's, it is unlikely that the more well-to-do will support such compensatory programs for the poor. Despite their rising levels of living, the expectations of the middle classes are likely to grow faster than their realizations. Rising incomes will be tested against rising standards. When the median family income reaches $25,000, as it is expected to in the year 2000, families with only $15,000 incomes will feel just as deprived as those with $6,000 incomes do today; and families with $25,000 incomes will note that many of their neighbors are better off than themselves.[20] In addition to rising expectations, increasing costs of education, medical care, and taxes will cramp family budgets. A Harvard study suggests that the costs of constructing highways, pipelines, schools, and other amenities in spreading suburbs will make suburban taxes rise faster than suburban incomes.[21] Not only rising yearly costs of higher education, but lengthening periods of college attendance will cut into the income and savings of a growing proportion of the nation's families.

Thus, affluence may rub in new sores of inequality rather than assuage them. With rising expectations and costs, the well-to-do will feel too "poor" to accept willingly the demands of the poor for the better housing, better schools, and better services, which would help to reduce inequalities. The nation's slow acceptance of such policies, combined with the increasing sensitivity and impatience of those lagging behind, will intensify the heat of inequality issues.

IMPLICATIONS

Much disturbance will be produced by the absence of inequality reduction. During the 1970's, there will be greater sensitivity to the inequalities between blacks and whites, between rich and poor, between center cities and suburbs, between the bottom and top half, and between regions of the United States. The issues of race and poverty will be clearly exhibited as questions of reduction of inequality rather than as problems of attaining a higher absolute level of living.

We expect greater sensitivity to inequalities because concern about the distribution of societal benefits increases with rising standards of living. In periods of depression and in low-income nations, the poor man sees that most are poor, but in periods of rising affluence, the poor man stands alone. Well-to-do by the standards of the past, he lags behind in the present.

The poor are also likely to be more disturbed about

inequality. They will be more aware that resources are not distributed on the basis of chance or individual effort alone, that the United States economy can be and is increasingly manipulated toward one kind of distribution or another, toward one kind of output or another. In addition, they will discover that despite the expanding economy, their share of the national income has not increased since World War II. Inequality will be indicted as the source of many of the nation's social ills. The economic return to different occupations and enterprises will be hard to explain on grounds of contribution to societal well-being. Limited chances of earning high or even adequate incomes because of mishaps of birth in the South or in rural areas will be assailed. The poor will learn that in the expanding economy some redistribution of resources would greatly help them without much loss to those who are more well-to-do. This situation contrasts with that of 1929, when redistribution would have helped those at the bottom very little. Consequently, those who are lagging behind are likely to conclude that the current distribution of resources *cannot* be defended on a self-evident basis of economic rationality and distributive justice.

The growing recognition of inequality will not automatically produce a solution to the problem. Rather it will initiate disturbing debate. The reduction of inequalities is unlikely to proceed smoothly in the 1970's. It will be a complicated, perhaps often violent, set of events, with only a minimum likelihood of suc-

223

cess unless a radical reorienting of American priorities prevails.

NOTES

1. We are using the percentage of total money income received by the bottom fifth of the population as our measure of inequality. U.S. Bureau of the Census, *Income Distribution in the United States* by H. P. Miller, 1960 Census Monograph (Washington, D.C.: U.S. Government Printing Office, 1966), p. 21; Gabriel Kolko, *Wealth and Power in America* (New York: Frederick A. Praeger, 1962), p. 14; George Soule, *Planning U.S.A.* (New York: The Viking Press, 1967), p. 62.
2. Marvin Friedman, "The Changing Profile of the Labor Force," *The American Federationist*, LXXIV, No. 7 (July 1967), 7.
3. The projections made by the National Commission on Technology, Automation, and Economic Progress and included in Table 12–1 assume a national unemployment rate of 3 per cent in 1975.
4. U.S. Department of Labor, "Employment of High School Graduates and Dropouts in 1964," *Special Labor Force Report*, No. 54 (June 1965), pp. A7, A8.
5. Friedman, *op. cit.*, p. 8.
6. *The New York Times*, June 5, 1967, p. 43.
7. Dorothy K. Newman, "The Decentralization of Jobs," *Monthly Labor Review* (May 1967). Currently it would cost a worker in Harlem $40 a month to commute by public transportation to work in an aircraft plant in

Farmingdale, L.I., in a parts plant in Yonkers, West-chester, or in a basic chemical plant on Staten Island.

8. Cf. William D. Hartley, "The Shape of the Future," *The Wall Street Journal,* December 27, 1966.

9. U.S. Department of Health, Education and Welfare, *Digest of Educational Statistics, 1968 Edition* (Washington, D.C.: U.S. Government Printing Office, 1968), p. 9, table 9; U.S. Bureau of the Census, *Current Population Reports,* Population Estimates, Ser. P-25, No. 305 (April 15, 1965).

10. U.S. Bureau of the Census, *Current Population Reports,* Table A.

11. U.S. Bureau of the Census, *Current Population Reports,* Population Estimates, Ser. P-25, No. 338 (May 31, 1966), p. 4, table 1. (Relates to the civilian noninstitutional population.)

12. See "The Credentials Trap," in S. M. Miller and Frank Riessman, eds., *Social Class and Social Policy* (New York: Basic Books, Inc., 1968).

13. This issue involves both the relevancy and authenticity of institutions of higher education today. These questions are discussed further in the section on "authenticity and purpose." Currently, colleges are not even giving much remedial assistance to low-income students, let alone devoting attention to the basic structural changes which are required in order to be relevant to students, whether they be wealthy or poor. In a study of 159 integrated colleges and universities, the Southern Education Association found that only twenty made any systematic effort to assist low-income students through preparatory, guidance, or tutoring programs or allowances in the curriculum; only six to eight in-

stitutions worked with students who were unquestion-
ably high risks. Black and student pressure may force
the majority of universities to join these few in
adequately assisting high risk students. John Egerton,
Higher Education for "High Risk" Students (Atlanta,
Ga.: Southern Education Association, 1968). Cf. The
Carnegie Commission on Higher Education, *Quality
and Equality: New Levels of Federal Responsibility
for Higher Education* (New York: McGraw-Hill Book
Co., 1968).

14. A *meritocracy* refers to a state in which position is
allocated solely on the basis of developed intellectual
ability. Michael Young, *The Rise of the Meritocracy*
(Baltimore, Md.: Penguin Books, Inc., 1958).

15. Christopher Jencks and David Riesman, *The Academic
Revolution* (Garden City, N.Y.: Doubleday Company,
Inc., 1968).

16. *The Report of the National Advisory Commission on
Civil Disorders* (New York: Bantam Books, 1968).
Many businesses located in central city areas are also
seeking programs to meet the needs of center-city
residents so as to prevent greater violence.

17. Michael S. March, "Federal Programs for Human Resources Development," *Federal Programs for the Development of Human Resources: A Compendium of
Papers* (The Joint Economic Committee, 90th Congress, 2nd Session, 1968), vols. 1 & 2, Appendix: "Public
Programs for the Poor."

18. For example, many middle- and upper-middle-income
children attended Head Start programs which were
initially intended for the poor.

19. In 1964, the President's Council of Economic Advisors

stated their opinion that economic expansion reduces inequalities by generating jobs for those who would otherwise be unemployed. We believe that although the absolute standard of living of the bottom 20 per cent rises in the periods of economic expansion, growth alone does not guarantee a rise *relative* to the standards of the rest of the population unless expansion rates are very high.

20. Ben Wattenberg and Richard M. Scammon, *This U.S.A.* (Garden City, N.Y.: Doubleday & Co., 1965), pp. 32. The $25,000 estimate is based on the assumption that family income will continue to increase at the 1950–1960 rate of 37 per cent.

21. Regional Plan Association, *Spread City: Projections of Development Trends and the Issues They Pose, 1960–1985* (New York: Regional Plan Association, 1965), p. 31.

13
Government, Freedom, and Purpose: Emerging Issues

Socialists don't claim to be able to make the world perfect; they claim to be able to make it better. And any thinking socialist will concede to the Catholic that when economic injustice has been negated, the fundamental problem of man's place in the universe will still remain. But what the socialist does claim is that the problem cannot be dealt with while the average human being's preoccupations are necessarily economic. It is all summed up in Marx's saying that after socialism has arrived, human history can begin.

George Orwell, *Collected Essays*

As Americans achieve what they personally feel is a satisfactory level of living, they turn their attention and energy from striving for material goods to questioning how they live and the purposes for which they live. In the 1970's and 1980's this questioning will be evident among not only relatively small groups of students, intellectuals, and social activists, but among broad sectors of the population. The questioning will focus on issues of governing, the balance between freedom and control, and authenticity and purpose. In this chapter we shall sketch the contours of these developing issues.

GOVERNING

The public affairs of the American people are managed by some 175,000 different governments—Federal, State, and local. In addition, many of the governments have separate departments working more or less independently on various kinds of public service. The chance for confusion, cross-purposes and wasted effort is almost limitless.[1]

Since 1937, when Louis Wirth wrote these words, the number of private as well as public, local, state, regional, and federal organizations governing the affairs of the American people has multiplied. The resulting structure of government—multileveled, overlapping, peculiarly dispersed—is clearly a major problem of American society. In addition to the problems of government coordination that have been inherited from the past, structural incoherencies arise as a result of the rapid expansion of communities and as a consequence of the powerful defenders of laissez faire who

229

effectively shun coordinated governmental efforts.

At the local level, the continuous growth of metropolitan areas further antiquates old political jurisdictions. The separation of suburban and city districts drains the city of many political leaders, as well as financial resources, and creates costly duplications in water-purification plants and numerous other community facilities that could be provided more efficiently on a metropolitan basis.

At the federal level, the nation's hesitancy to accept a coordinated system of planning and allocation has led to a situation where the planning measures of government agencies are conducted ad hoc, unconnected with the efforts of other agencies or other levels of government.[2] The Nixon solution is to decrease the federal role in programs and to use the federal government primarily as a revenue receiver, which will disburse funds to states with little control over their use.

This solution, like others, runs into the problem that all levels of government suffer from the limited ability to make and implement decisions. The American governmental structure increasingly is faced with its incapacity to move. At one time the centralization of agencies is advised in the hope of gaining control and coordination; at other times, decentralization is offered as the solution. Without change in resources, styles and purposes, neither form seems to be successful.

VALUES

Even more disturbing than problems of decision-making, implementation, and coordination is the lack of deep political debate concerning the goals and value bases of government action. Planning and coordination are important only as instruments for achieving certain standards of well-being. They are not "social goods" in and of themselves: they must serve a purpose. Social policy does not consist simply of technical rules for implanting value-neutral hardware. The crucial questions remain: How do we define a *good society?* Toward what ends are we planning? We lack agreement, and a difficult-to-use structure complicates the policy choices.

But even greater efficiency and effectiveness cannot solve the problems of government policy. Many more resources are needed for socially useful ends. But these additional resources will not be easy to gain. A major problem of public governments is that American citizens do not recognize that their affluence is more a result of the expansion of the economy than of their increased individual competence, ability, and education. The recent rapid growth of the income levels of professionals, for example, owes more to the expanding demand for professional services than to the improving competence of professionals. Until Americans recognize that a major source of their well-being springs from manipulated and engineered affluence, there will be reluctance to expand the public sector to the levels

231

required to provide the goods and services needed in the 1970's. Reevaluations are sorely needed of the sources of well-being and of the responsibilities individuals have to their society and to the less fortunate at home and abroad.

PROFESSIONALISM

The issues of government organization and resources have been disturbing for a long time. However, a new issue of great significance is emerging. It is the widespread questioning of the representativeness of democratic society and the usefulness of the grievance-and-change mechanisms of highly bureaucratized activities.[3] This questioning will rise sharply during the 1970's because private and public bureaucracies will increasingly affect individuals' lives, because these institutions appear to grow more anonymous as they grow larger and more complex, and because new expectations for democracy grow with society's rising level of educational attainment. The issue of the relationship between bureaucracies and citizens will have three major aspects: professional responsiveness, citizen participation, and pluralistic representation.

During the 1970's, the continuing tension between the public responsibility of professions and the internal development of professions will become increasingly significant as the activities of professionals and social scientists assume greater importance in affecting persons' daily lives. Individual clients and groups will demand greater professional responsiveness to their needs.[4] The conflict created by these demands will be most acute in education and the social services, but it will also be important in many other fields, especially in economic decisions.

The lack of professional responsiveness to clients is part of the general problem of the role of professionals and professionalism within society. Periodically, there is a push toward increasing professionalization as the answer to the problems of developing competence, commitment, and decent services. One result is that the profession emphasizes its *own* standards and tends to build its independence by isolating or insulating itself from the larger society. Efforts to make private professions accountable to consumers or public representatives often mean unreasonable and undesirable interference. On the other hand, the independence of professionals can result in the dominance of guild rather than public concerns, leading to the neglect of the broad needs of the majority of those who purportedly are to be served.

In some fields, not only the introduction of new constraints on professional behavior but the reorganization of services will be necessary to meet public needs. For example, decentralization of big city school systems may be necessary for programs to be adequately geared to the needs of children and for the development of better parent-school relations. It is also doubtful whether desirable standards of health care can be provided for all without considerable reorganization of the medical

233

services. As pointed out in Chapter 5, both the size and the distribution of medical manpower need *public* attention. Between 1950 and 1961, despite the fact that a rising percentage of the gross national product was devoted to medical care, the population per physician remained nearly constant.[5]

Although the size and distribution of the health force and the distribution of the costs of training and maintaining this force are issues which affect the entire public, well-organized professional interests generally have prevented them from being treated directly as political issues. Citizens of the 1970's will be increasingly dissatisfied with the quality of their medical services and will likely force these issues into the political arena. Extensive government programs will be required if an adequate number of physicians and other medical personnel are to be trained and effectively deployed to meet the increased medical needs of the growing population, as well as the needs of regions which currently have a severe shortage of health personnel.

REPRESENTATION

Structural reorganization of services and individual efforts on the part of professionals and experts to be more responsive to clients are sorely needed, but they will not guarantee representation of citizens' interests. Nor will they allow citizens to feel that they can plan their lives without having to depend fatalistically upon

234

the distant actions of professionals, experts, and bureaucratic agencies.

These needs, as discussed earlier in Chapter 7, have given rise to the demand for "no services without representation." One segment of this demand was incorporated in the notion of maximum feasible participation of the poor, introduced in the 1964 Economic Opportunity Act. In the coming years the nonpoor as well as the poor will be actively concerned about maximum feasible participation. Citizens will demand to be involved in pending decisions, rather than being informed of already-made decisions. They will declare their right to a voice in the character and dispensation of social services and education.

A new set of government leaders, including blacks, Puerto Ricans, students, and other minority groups, will not be enough to satisfy these demands. Although a transfer of power to new leaders is important and is slowly taking place, new relationships between the leaders and those they lead, between the organs of government and the citizens, are required. There will be public pressure for professionals and public agencies to make the transfer of power to those who have been deprived of it also a road to *the transformation of power*. The agencies, the professionals, and the experts of the welfare state and of private bureaucracies will no longer be able to rest behind barriers of tradition, political protection, or professional competence, and assert their independence from the persons who depend upon them for succor or advance.

235

What are the broad implications of these issues concerning the governing of society? We believe the thesis of "the end of ideology" applies at least as well to liberal ideology as to the exhaustion of the Marxist heritage of the nineteenth century. The student and the black challenges of the 1960's can be seen as an indictment of the received liberal wisdom about the representativeness and pluralism of democratic society, the openness of society to deviant behavior, and the usefulness of the grievance-and-change mechanism of highly bureaucratic activities.[6] Liberal ideology is under attack for not accurately describing the working of society, for overestimating the adaptability of "the system," for underestimating its punitiveness, and for misreading its representative character. This criticism is not likely to die rapidly, especially where agencies and policies are slow to change. Consequently, the legitimacy of many governmental actions will be challenged, and social unrest will continue.

FREEDOM AND CONTROL

DEVIANCE

The concern with social deviance has been a central thread in discussions of social problems. Deviance will continue to be an issue in the future but in a new way. What appear to be issues of personal deviance are to some extent challenges to the functioning of liberal society. In part, these challenges appear as civil lib-

236

erties issues; in part, as the questioning of the norms and goals of society; and, in part, as an assessment of the functioning of society. The developing issue underlying social deviance is not the sociologist's concern with social disorganization, but rather the extent to which society is willing to countenance actions that major groups consider deviant. Perhaps it would be better to think in terms of disturbing acts and reactions to them, rather than in terms of a consensus of norms and values and deviants from them. The disturbers frequently oppose the consensus, rather than stray from it.

The fragile dialectical balance between social stability and personal autonomy tilts first one way, then the other. Yearly, the interdependent bureaucratic structures of society increase in size, complexity, and frequently in power. Formal means of control continuously conflict with personal norms, and the rules of bureaucracies jut into the practices of numerous small groups and communities. Within the next decade, the rights of individuals in the face of often well-meaning but nonetheless arbitrary and oppressive private and public bureaucracies will be a major legal issue as well as a social issue. The very institutions, such as government agencies and universities, that are constructed to benefit individuals simultaneously deprive them of their freedom.[7]

Deviants or disturbers who are harming no one are frequently unable to escape the attacks of major groups. The houses of hippies are raided for the evidences of

237

"grass" by police departments that are too "busy" to answer burglary calls in less than ten minutes. Early in the morning, 200 policemen invade the rooms of sleeping students at a large university to arrest 38 of them. Male students are dismissed by high schools for wearing long hair, even though it is neat and clean; coeds are dismissed or placed on probation by colleges for daring to sleep off campus. "Midnight raids" are conducted on homes of families receiving Aid to Dependent Children to see if there is a "man in the house" who could or should be contributing to the support of the children.[8]

Many feel that society should not only sporadically govern individual behavior in matters such as these, but also should continuously govern individual acts that are felt by majority groups to be deviant or harmful, as was done during the prohibition period of the 1920's.

Despite these organized controls, the range of many freedoms in society does appear to be expanding. As societal symbols of affluence and success have lost much of their meaning, many have been freed from the bonds which striving for these symbols entails. With their new freedom, these individuals are beginning to experiment with some new and some very old forms of living, which are classed as deviant by majority groups. They contest the illegitimacy of some forms of grievance and protest, they seek independence and autonomy.

The extent to which our society can permit questioning of the legitimacy of political structures and the

238

violation of laws will be a continuing issue. The great importance of the police today is more because of their social-control activity than because of their anticrime pursuits.[9] In turn, police behavior rather than the originating acts, become the issue, indicating the difficulties in the opening up of society and in containing these openings.

As new generations push forward, trying to experiment and to develop new freedoms, while others in society feel obligated to provide leadership and constraints, tensions will arise at the interpersonal level as well as at the legislative and administrative levels of society. The issues of autonomy are not only questions of law, as in the regulation of the use of drugs, but are questions of public attitudes. These attitudes affect the way in which dissenters and deviants are treated by others. How a junior high school youth with long hair is treated by his crew-cut peers (or the way the crew-cut youth is treated by his long-haired peers), or how demonstrators are treated by bystanders and even by those demonstrating against them are important tests of freedom and the strength of the liberal society.

The conflict between promoting or accepting differences and disagreements, on the one hand, and social convergence and stability, on the other, is not easily resolved. In the 1960's, the tension grew between the freedom to dissent and the desire for social control and limitations on behavior. In the 1970's this conflict will be more strenuous. We seem to be in a watershed period, where many different streams (for example,

239

civil rights protest, student unrest, the closing down of some of the cold war forms, the emergence of a "kick culture") contribute to breaking through old styles and contesting traditional practices. The ability of agencies to respond creatively rather than reflexively to these pressures appears limited.

AUTHENTICITY AND PURPOSE

We have discussed amenities, inequality, personal freedom, and power. While the nature of these issues will change in the future, they are already part of the rhetoric of politics and public policy in the United States. In the next decades, we believe that the issues of authenticity and purpose will emerge as prominent new public concerns.[10]

The issues have been treated to date as intergenerational conflict between those under and over thirty years old. To interpret the issues as merely problems of growing up banalizes them, because many of these issues, molded by the events of succeeding years, will long be public concerns in this country and elsewhere. Economic advance, even the more equitable spread of affluence, will be increasingly challenged as the primary objective of society. As Arthur Schlesinger, Jr., has argued, it is not that material issues no longer are important, but that the diminution of some problems of the absolute level of living and the vast new possibilities of the economy open up questions of not only who

240

shall benefit, but toward what ends should the cornu-copia be directed?[11] The refrain of suburban sadness, the pathos of the empty American life, the attack upon mass society, although undoubtedly exaggerated and partially misleading, are symptomatic of the concern of an affluent society that is deficient in its quality of life. The denunciation of society by the beatniks, hippies, and yippies, the search for love power, and withdrawal are indications of society's failure to provide a feeling of authenticity.

Alone, neither growing economic affluence nor politi-cal democracy constitute the *good* society. Despite their important contributions to well-being, they do not end social problems; they change them. The question "What lies beyond affluence?" will be recurrently raised.

We believe that in the future the issues of authen-ticity and purpose will be fused to a greater extent than they are today. People will increasingly discover that each without the other is incomplete; purpose without authenticity in relations can lead to harsh authoritar-ianism, while authenticity without purpose can become a precious and fragile egoism, ignoring the anguish of the many.

We do not pretend to have an adequate classification of the disturbing feelings that will arise about the quality of life, but we believe the following concerns will grow:

1. *The quality of human relations:* The attacks on commercialization, competitiveness, and banality will

SOCIAL POLICIES OF THE FUTURE

deepen. The treatment of individuals as things, as means, and the neutral, unaffective interactions among individuals, and the effort to limit social science to cognitive rationality are part of this concern.

2. *Black-white relationships:* Hopefully we shall reduce material inequalities between blacks and whites in this society, but as we do the issue will increasingly become the nature of the relations between black and white. The easy slogans of "tolerance," "intergroup relations," and even "integration" and "pluralist society," not to speak of "assimilation" and "accommodation," are proving and will increasingly prove to be inadequate. The quality of black-white relationships, coming to see one another as persons, will be a long-time struggle for a society that first embraced racism and then comfortably denied its existence.

3. *The discovery and realization of self:* An increasing segment of the population is being freed from having to do meaningless work in order to obtain the necessities of life. Growing numbers of professional people can now choose or shape their work so as to pursue in their occupations the goals and activities which in past generations they would have been restricted to pursuing in a few leisure hours. As they discover this new freedom, they are faced with the responsibility of finding their own "thing" and doing it. The personal goals of success and even achievement are not enough for many. They are infused with a

desire to be part of and committed to a larger social purpose. Much of the appeal of the near-mythology of the "third world" springs from the possibility of commitment to a purpose which is more profound than that of expanding the affluence of the already affluent.

4. *Alienation in work:* The classic Marxist concern with alienation from work is having a strong effect on the majority of the population, who will not have acquired the freedom to choose the work they do in their jobs, and among the growing minority who see their chores as not offering possibilities of serious involvement in useful tasks. The rat-race of work, the avoidance of meaningful relations among workers, and the discontinuities between work and the rest of life will be problems for many. Money abates alienation; it does not overcome it. Leisure connoisseurship can only partially compensate for work discontent.

5. *Campus relationships:* Many students' moral outrage against the university, the institution which most affects them, only partially represents a demand for the right to participate in decisions affecting them. Beyond the cry for *student power,* students are seeking an end to hypocrisy and to inauthentic relationships, both within the university and in the world into which they must someday graduate. Many are no longer willing to accept pat establishment answers to why there are slums, why there are wars, why superordinates suppress subordinates, even within the university, and why

higher education consists more of filling out forms and attempting to outmanipulate one's manipulators than learning which is relevant to and engaged in mutually by professors and students. These concerns will not be short-lived. Today's students are unlikely to be "bought off" by affluence following graduation. Many are likely to continue to attack what they see as wrong and false in society and to couple their attacks with more clear-cut visions.

6. *Morality and antihypocrisy:* The Nuremberg and Eichmann trials provide the institutional basis for anger at immorality, masquerading as bureaucratic conformity, and at hypocrisy, dancing in the veils of "reality." The message of the trials, the responsibility each individual has for his own actions in the face of monolithic bureaucratic structures, as well as in one-to-one relationships, has become immediate to many youths and sensitive adults in America. As individuals, very shortly after the trials, not only did they have to assess the actions of others, but they had to choose their own course of action with respect to Vietnam, either acting upon or adopting what they had stated to be the responsibility of all men. The concept of responsibility, of the burden of moral man in an immoral society, is asserted today. A thirst for morality in politics, perhaps excessively righteous, is developing and will not easily be quenched.

This catalog of issues does not represent good against evil, although some fall into that perspective, but rather

new searchings in a society where *gemeinschaft* is com-
mercialized into *pseudo-gemeinschaft* and *morality* is
transmuted into a *higher morality* which transcends
people. Nor are these concerns based on the notion of
Paradise Lost—that in the dim past, innocence, whole-
ness, and goodness pervaded the earth, only to disappear with the coming of industrial man. The order
and castes of feudalism constrained the majority; rural
man not only communed with nature but was consigned
by its capricious rule to a life of uncertainty and threat.
War and brutality as well as cooperation and human-
ness existed. Some who grieve about American society
bear witness to its golden past, but for increasing numbers the issue is not the recovering of a dubious past
but the achievement of new goals which freedom from
economic danger and nature's ravages makes possible.

These issues will be public concerns; however, contrary to the common American fallacy that for every
problem there is a solution, usually a law, they may not
be amenable to governmentally contrived resolutions.
The lack of authenticity and purpose from which American society has long been suffering will not be easily
affected by public policy. Rather there will be recurring
questioning of how the population will individually accept alternative approaches to life, new norms of organizational behavior, and new patterns of relationships
among individuals. Legislation may respond to these
issues, as, for example, in the assertion that *selective*
conscientious objection on the basis of one's moral feeling about a war be permitted; however, its role will be
much smaller than in the distribution of amenities or

even in the transfer and transformation of political power.

"OPT-OUTS"

The center of questioning concerning authenticity and purpose is likely to fluctuate between the individual and political action, between individuals giving up and leaving society and individuals pursuing collective action in an effort to shape the society. Among individuals' responses to these urgings will be *counterculture, familism,* and *collegiality.*

The counterculture approach consciously chooses to "opt out" of contemporary patterns. There are many variants: a significant but temporary mode for a few will be communitarian units, such as those suggested by Paul Goodman. When politics appear unuseful, ineffective, immoral, then counterculture and individualistic responses expand.

When new politics of hope, change, and commitment exist, solutions may be sought in the larger world of affluence. The effort will be to offset inauthenticity in the larger society rather than to insulate oneself from that society. Some forms of this effort have emerged in the reappearance of familism, an ideology in which the family provides love and protection and demands high allegiance and commitment. Another mode is political commitment, in which morality is demanded in both means and ends, a straining request in all areas of life, but especially where politics has been conceptualized

246

as "the art of the possible." The McCarthy campaign of 1968 brought many of the disaffected at least temporarily into the political action realm.

In work situations, there will be increasing call for the spread of collegiality rather than for hierarchy. The professional-academic model of peer relations has been cited as not only productive of morale but of productivity. It is currently pushed in settings such as research laboratories, but it will probably be sought in an expanding number of other work settings with highly educated personnel. Certainly it is being demanded by many students within the university.

The solution of changing society from the inside, in contrast to the counterculture response, builds norms and patterns to offset the excessive demands of economism—the values of efficiency and of economic growth. It involves the collective discovery that affluence alone is not enough, and that society must look at its morality as well as at its money. The implicit hierarchy of societal goals is shifting from society as a handmaiden of the economy to the economy as part of the society in which individual members are sensitive to one another.

With this shift, the fragility of society comes from two directions. It comes from those seekers of authenticity who remain in society, questioning it, attempting to change it, and then, sometimes in a near-solipsistic desperation, violently reacting against the society and its symbols of inauthenticity. It also springs from the authoritarian reaction, stirred by the challenge of protest but with hardier roots, which produces counter-violence. As the old majorities break down in society, violence represents the reaction of newly rising groups to inauthenticity and the reaction of older groups to the challenge to established norms.

The issue of authenticity does not represent only a psychological struggle of the young. It is an issue over which the stability of the entire society may shake. Paul Johnson has fervently projected the broad importance of the 1968 revolt of French students:

What is the point of improving the structure of higher education by reformism, if the rest of society remains the same? Paris University, for instance, can now churn out 5,000 sociologists a year. They are, of course, taught in a silly way. But supposing you revolutionize their teaching, you are still left with the problem of what they are to do in the world outside. The cleverer ones become teachers, and churn out more sociologists; the others become public relations advisors in factories, and suchlike, or scrabble around to get a toehold in another profession; at worst, flunkeys, at best, privileged acolytes serving the altars of capitalism, helping to buttress a rotten society which pursues consumption for its own sake.

Can you reform the medical school without at the same time questioning the assumptions on which the medical profession is organized and the functions of medicine in society? How to "improve" science courses without at the same time asking what science is supposed to do for mankind? Can you replan the Political Science Faculty without at the same time replanning the political system? After all, the university is

248

the matrix of society, the institution which produces its elites, assumptions and objectives. Will a *real* reform of the matrix be permitted, entailing as it must the eventual transformation of the adult world. . . . I hasten to add that the students cannot produce all the answers (or rather, they produce a bewildering variety of them). But they are asking questions which have never been posed before in the context of a political offensive, and with a stridency which makes it impossible for their elders to brush them aside.[12]

The validity of all of Johnson's judgments is not the issue, but whether or not students are raising questions of broad and continuing significance. Politically and socially, the questions of authenticity and purpose will be serious issues of the next decades.

CONCLUSION

Since social problems have traditionally focused on such tangibles as crime or mental illness, it may be disturbing to treat such amorphous issues as authenticity, inequality, and the balance between individual freedom and social stability as social problems. The knowing answers which social science has offered for its traditional social problems are inapplicable. Frequently, the goals are the issue, rather than the choice of a means to "solve" a problem. In a sense, there is not even a resolution but only a temporary handling of many problems, alleviating some tensions while building up others. But if a sociology of social problems is to

249

be relevant to the broad issues of society, it can neither be relegated to the "easy to touch and analyze," nor can it be a narrow preserve of the rejected topics of other social science specialties. That is why there is beginning to be a call for the resurrection of "political economy" which succumbed to the narrow professionalization of economics.

The emergence of planning and the conscientious structuring of society mean that the social sciences will face new expectations. In order to deal with the social problems of the future, sociology must refocus itself so that it will be able to think about the big problems of society, rather than being relegated to dealing, within society's perspective, with those who are found troubling.

In the decades ahead, American society will be confronted by the issues of amenities, distribution of resources, power, and, yes, the quality of human relations. To comprehend these broad issues requires a theory of American society. Now that social science, and particularly the sociology of social problems, has moved beyond a cataloging of disturbing acts, its future development requires an understanding of the general changes in society.

In this book we have attempted to place immediate, disturbing problems in the context of the broad economic and social issues of the nation. The future of inequality depends on the general character of American society; a more equal society is not an engineering job of shoring up some defects in a stable edifice but

250

rather a value and structural task of constructing a new society in the 1970's, when an additional nation of 35 million persons will emerge with an additional gross national product of $400 billion.

The quality of what is to be distributed is always at issue as well as the equity of the shares. In 1980, the preceding decade will be judged not only on its material performance but also on the quality of life it engendered. If this book has been uneasy about the future, it is because both material and qualitative gains are our agenda, especially for the poor and discriminated against but for all Americans as well. American possibilities are great. A concentrated will is necessary if they are to be realized.

New political stirrings offer hope. The pessimism of the late 1960's stressed the immovability of society. We are more optimistic about the general changes which may occur in society during the 1970's and 1980's. There are important signs that new kinds of political movements are developing which can begin to push the kinds of programs of economic and social change outlined here.

Change is possible because the issues we have discussed are becoming clear-cut and obvious. It does not require great insight to be able to state the issues as we have. They are already emerging clearly and politically in the American scene, so that they become even more politicized and rally more people to pushing along these lines.

Second, an important step has been taken in the

attack on the Pentagon, the military-industrial complex, and the Vietnam War. All these steps are indications of the possibility of drastic change in foreign and military policies, opening up the likelihood of great shifts in American public expenditures. The groups that have fought against the military outlook of the United States and its foreign-policy corollaries can now move together toward other kinds of goals of great internal significance.

Third, student and black unrest has shown the extent of dismay and the need for change in the society.

Fourth, the Kennedy and McCarthy movements and the little-noticed achievements of the 1968 Democratic Convention lead to the conclusion that there are important, sizable groups of voters who seek change.

What has been missing is an ideology, a point of view, a platform, or a program. What we have heard are revolutionary tactics without revolutionary goals, and the reiteration of liberal objectives without recognition of their failure. What we are suggesting is a radical restructuring capable of appealing to a large number of voters who feel the need for change and do not see the possibility of a politically viable program. A reallocation of American wealth to meet a reasonable set of priorities, a redistribution of goods and power to benefit the bottom half of the population, and a concern for moral purpose implied in these changes could coalesce a powerful political force grappling with the issues of the 1970's.

NOTES

1. Louis Wirth, "Localism, Regionalism, and Centralization," *American Journal of Sociology,* XLII (January 1937), 493.
2. Cf. Charles A. Reich, "The Law of the Planned Society," *Yale Law Journal,* LXXV, No. 8 (July 1966).
3. We do not restrict the discussion to government agencies, but include the nongovernmental agencies and organizations which disperse services and resources or which represent interest groupings. Political scientists have until recently been at great pains to insist that nongovernment activities are part of the governmental process. Cf. David B. Truman, *The Governmental Process* (New York: Alfred A. Knopf, Inc., 1951).
4. For discussions of the changing relationships between professionals and clients in commonweal or general welfare organizations, see H. Kaufman, "Emerging Conflicts in the Doctrines of Public Administration," *American Political Science Review,* L (1956), 1056–1073; Peter M. Blau and W. Richard Scott, *Formal Organizations: A Comparative Approach* (San Francisco, Calif.: Chandler Publishing Company, 1962), pp. 54–57; W. Richard Scott, "Theory of Organizations," in Robert E. L. Faris, ed., *Handbook of Modern Sociology* (Chicago: Rand McNally & Company, 1964), pp. 524–525.
5. U.S. National Commission on Technology, Automation and Economic Progress, *Report: Technology and the American Economy* (Washington, D.C.: U.S. Government Printing Office, February 1966), p. 78.
6. Cf. *The Report of the National Advisory Commission*

on Civil Disorders (New York: Bantam Books, 1968), which shows that contrary to the "riffraff theory" of riots, in the 1967 riots of six major cities, about 18 per cent of the residents in the areas participated in the disorders; the majority were employed and were representative of the adult population of the communities involved.

7. Cf. Charles A. Reich, "The New Property," *The Yale Law Journal*, LXXIII (April 1964), 783–787.

8. Cf. Charles A. Reich, "Individual Rights and Social Welfare: The Emerging Legal Issues," *The Yale Law Journal*, LXXIV (June 1965), 125.

9. The statement is not fully accurate since deviant or disturbing acts are frequently defined as criminal.

10. The terms *authenticity* and *purpose* do not adequately convey the issues we attempt to outline in this section. We recognize their deficiencies but plead that a major problem is the lack of open discussion of them by social scientists. We hope that others will further develop and refine them.

11. Arthur M. Schlesinger, Jr., "Where Does the Liberal Go From Here?" *The New York Times Magazine*, August 4, 1957.

12. Paul Johnson, "The New Spectre Haunting Europe," *The New Statesman*, LXXV, No. 1941 (May 24, 1969), 676.

Acknowledgments

We thank the American Academy of Arts and Sciences for permission to reprint passages from our paper, "Poverty: Changing Social Stratification," which was previously published in *On Understanding Poverty: Perspectives from the Social Sciences,* edited by Daniel Patrick Moynihan (New York: Basic Books, 1969); the American Academy of Political and Social Science for permission to reprint portions of our article "Poverty, Inequality and Conflict" (with Martin Rein and Bertram Gross), from *The Annals,* CCCLXXIII (September 1967); and the *Notre Dame Lawyer* and Edgar and Jean Cahn for permission to quote from Edgar S. Cahn and Jean C. Cahn, "What Price Justice: The Civilian Perspective Revisited," *Notre Dame Lawyer,* XLI, No. 6 (September 1966), 937–938.

Index

Index

Index

111; integration, 158; legal services, 103; in Mississippi, 142; occupational distribution, 127–128; participation in politics, 151; police protection, 98–99, 116; positive self-image, 172; recreational facilities, 100; rural vs. urban residence, 203; social mobility, 133–134; social prestige, 163, 164; and token leadership, 235; voting, 144, 145

neighborhood amenities, 14, 202, 203; fire protection, 98, 99; libraries and museums, 98, 100–101; police protection, 84, 85, 98–99; recreation facilities, 98, 99–100; sanitation services, 85, 98

Newman, Dorothy K. 117, 224

New York City, low-income housing admissions, 71–72, 81; welfare means tests, 165–166, 167

New York State, health services, 95; school expenditures, 123

Nichols, Robert C., 138

Nikias, Mata Kouvari, 92, 94, 113

Nixon, Richard M., 147, 167, 230

nonfarm poor, 35

nonincome compensation (*see* fringe benefits)

nonwhites, housing, 70; infant mortality rates, 93, 95–96; poverty, 30, 40, 46, 50, 61

Norway, income range in, 17

Nuremburg trials, 244

nutrition, 25, 28, 46, 97, 114, 207

occupational distribution: in center cities, vs. suburbs, 213;

effect of computer, 213–214; geographical shifts of jobs, 213; Negro, and job future, 211; 1949 vs. 1965, 210–211; nonwhite, and job future, 211; unskilled jobs, 211, 213, 214

occupational prestige, 163

Office of Economic Opportunity, 8, 59, 65, 104, 108, 109, 150, 235

Old Age Survivors, Disability, and Health Insurance (OASDI), benefits and cost-of-living index, 77

open enrollment, college, 201

operation bed check, 158–159, 238

operative workers, among poor, 41

Opler, M. K., 178

opt-outs, and authenticity, 246

Orden, Susan R., 177

Ornati, Oscar, 24, 46, 69, 71, 79, 109, 111, 113, 117

Orshansky, Mollie, 16, 25, 28, 31, 34, 35, 43, 47, 48, 49, 50, 83; on demography of poor, qt., 30–31; on SSA poverty line, qt., 7–8

Orwell, George, on socialism, qt., 228

Oshima, Harry T., 50

Ossowski, Stanislaw, 16, 18; on definition of class, qt., 5; on social class, qt., 18–19

parent-child groups, not on poverty roll, 31

parks, 98, 99, 100

Parsons, Talcott, 15, 17, 19; on Negro citizenship, qt., 158

ness, 171–172; and public policies, 219–220

services, basic, 12, 203; amenities or investments, 86; availability vs. delivery, 87–88; defined, 84–85; goals of, 86–87; health services, 91–97; legal services, 103–107, 117; mass transportation, 84, 85, 86, 89, 101–103, 117; need for funds, 107–108; neighborhood amenities, 84, 98–101; public vs. private, 85–86; social services, 84, 88–91, 235; Sweden vs. U.S., 85; and well-being, 10–11, 87, 107–108; yield from, 87

service workers, among poor, 41

Sewell, William H., 138

Sexton, Patricia, 116, 139; on recreational facilities, qt., 99

Shah, Vimal P., 138

Sheldon, E. B., 51

Siegel, Paul M., 174

Silver, Allan, 178

Smelser, Neal, 137

Smigel, Erwin O., 16

Smith, James D., 59, 65

Smolensky, Eugene, 45, 46

social change, and inequality, 191–194

social class, capitalistic, 18–19; and illness, 111–112

social deviance, future of, 236–240

social honor, 169, 170, 186, 214; defined, 161–162; discrimination, 162–163; vs. economic class, 162; and income, 164–165; negative income tax, 166–167; prestige, 9, 10, 17, 162,

163; and styles of life, 167, 168, 169; and welfare means tests, 165–166

social mobility, 12, 24, 182, 183; downward mobility, 133, 134, 140; and education, 119–121, 133–134, 200–201; and family status, 132–134; goals for, 134–136; and income, 57–60, 65–66, 133–134, 136; intergenerational vs. intragenerational, 131–132, 136; and Negro, 133, 134; in South, 141; stratum mobility, 132; and well-being, 120–121

social problems, 249–252; and social deviance, 236

social science, 185, 205; goals of, 183–184; and political issues, 168; and social problems, 249–252; and social theory, 15

Social Security Administration (SSA), 7–8, 13, 25, 26, 27, 28, 29, 30, 31, 35, 49, 50, 65, 165; negative income tax, 166–167; payments to aged, 82–83

social services, 84, 235; admission process, 88, 89; aftermath, 88, 91; completion process, 88, 89–90; and new dissidence, 240; presentation of programs, 88

social stability, and individual rights, 229, 239, 249

social theory, and social science, 15

sociology, 16

Soule, George, 224

South, migration from, 203, 223; and Negro education, 124; Negro suffrage, 144; poverty,